REDWOOD WRITING PROJECT

"My Trouble Is My English"

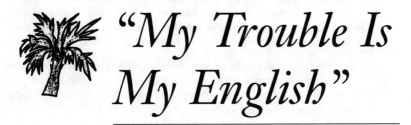

"My Trouble Is My English"

Asian Students and the American Dream

Danling Fu

Boynton/Cook Publishers
HEINEMANN
Portsmouth, NH

Boynton/Cook Publishers, Inc.
A subsidiary of Reed Elsevier Inc.
361 Hanover Street, Portsmouth, NH 03801-3912
Offices and agents throughout the world

Consulting Editor: Tom Newkirk
Production: J. B. Tranchemontagne
Cover design: Darci Mehall

Library of Congress Cataloging-in-Publication Data
Fu, Danling.
   "My trouble is my English" : Asian students and the American dream / Danling Fu.
      p.   cm.
   Includes bibliographical references.
   ISBN 0-86709-355-2
   1. English language—Study and teaching—Oriental speakers.
2. English philology—Study and teaching—United States. 3. Asian Americans—Education—Language arts. 4. Asian students—United States. 5. Asian American students. I. Title.
PE1130.A2F8 1995
428'.007—dc20   94–44918
                                                                   CIP

Printed in the United States of America on acid-free paper
99 98 97 96 95   **DA**   1 2 3 4 5 6 7 8 9

To Maryellen H. Mefford

Without her, I would not have become what I am today.

Contents

Foreword

"My Trouble Is My English" is written from the inside. Danling Fu, the author, knows firsthand what it is to learn English and experience the isolation of a new culture, as well as to apply an objective lens to our system of education in America. This is a fast read of a complex subject, the literacy and acculturation of Asian students within the American high school. Although the focus of this book is on Asian students in the same family, we see more than their struggle to acquire English. We see school, family, and culture through the eyes of the students, as well as through the critical eye of Danling Fu.

We get a glimpse of the rapidly growing under-class, lower-track students in the high school. Her data show that the approaches used to help these students actually maintain their isolation and insure against any upward mobility in our society.

This is a timely book about the most rapidly growing body of students in the country, those whose first language is not English. By the year 2000, students new to English will dominate our schools. Unless we begin today to understand how to work with new cultures, including our own lower-track students, we will be buried in our own ignorance, and lose out on the riches of the new pluralism in our society. *"My Trouble Is My English"* opens the door to this new understanding.

This is no distant look at the problem of literacy and acculturation. Danling Fu spent a full year at the high school that she studied. She helped teach the students, observed them in cafeterias and assemblies, attended their classes, went to their homes, and ate their food. Further, they visited her home and attended various community events together. She unlaces our convenient stereotypes about Asians, our views of them as "ethnic species," by portraying the different aspirations of each student as well as their individual approaches to learning.

Danling moves close to the instructional scene. Her lens focuses on the worksheets intended to lift the students' skills. Through both observation and interview she shows the students' confusion when using them. The lower the track in which students are placed, the less they discuss. Sadly, teachers interpret the silence of Asian and other students as their being slow and unable to think. Danling rightfully argues that limited English-speaking students need to talk in order to connect with others, to understand the people around them, and to explore the knowledge in the world they have come to join.

Her cases are hard-working students pressured into filling blanks with words they do not understand. We observe the students' breathless entry into the ESL room, anxious for help with homework that does not help them learn to read or write English. They struggle to pass daily work that is beyond them. ESL teachers, including the author, are frustrated by the pace of the system as well as their limited access to the students. Clearly, these students needed more help with their English and a different system of learning in the classroom where the ESL room and content teachers would have worked together.

Although this is not a book spelling out the details of how to teach non-English-speaking students, there are just enough instances of strong teaching, some intentional, some accidental, that a scaffold for helping non-English-speaking students becomes clear. Assignments that draw on the students' background in Laos bring forth coherent, written stories. In one instance an assignment elicited artwork that allowed both the teacher and the class to begin to understand Laotian culture. Blanks demanding single-word answers confuse the students, yet responses demanding more writing through open-ended assignments aid them.

At times this is a very sad book. The school seldom places itself in the student's position. The richness of Asian culture enters the school only by accident. Other times, there is humor. One of the older boys signed up for a music class because he wished to learn how to write songs as he did in

Laos. His teacher was puzzled by his request; she had never been asked by a student for help in writing music. Again, the notion of authorship, and the chance to express and contribute, is thwarted.

Educators need this book to assist students who are disconnected from their education. We need this book as a fundamental document to help non-English-speaking students as well as to reconsider learning in the American high school. Further, we need someone who is new to our culture to remind us of the contradictions between school structure and our democratic heritage, as well as those instances when students meld their cultures and dreams with new opportunity in America.

Donald H. Graves

Acknowledgments

This book represents my transformation from a semi-feudal educator to a democratic teacher. Many teachers told me that they were born as whole language teachers. Certainly I was not. For the first seven years of my teaching in China, I taught my students exactly how I was taught—drill them with grammar patterns and phonics, quiz them every week on spelling words, drown them with tons of worksheets, bore them with analysis of every word in a sentence. I was always proud of my toughness and believed in "spare the rod, spoil the child."

Then my study in America helped me realize that my teaching style treated my students not as intelligent human beings but as senseless robots. This realization didn't happen overnight, or after reading a few books or attending a few workshops, but through many years of study and discussion among colleagues and research in real classroom settings. It is this real literate community that reshaped me, reeducated me, and transformed me into the educator I am today.

My first thanks go to a community formed by my former professors and colleagues: Donald Graves, Jane Hansen, Thomas Newkirk, Patricia Sullivan, Bud Khleif, Thomas Schram, Donald Murray, Sue Ducharme, Nancy Herdecker, Kay Morgan, Bonnie Sunstein, Dan Seger, Peg Murray, Ann Vibert, Mary Comstock, Judy Fueyo, Cindy Matthews, Peg Voss, Jay Simmons, Tom Romano, Elizabeth Chiseri-Strater, Donna Qualey, JoAnn Curtis, Carol Wilcox, and Ralph Fletcher. Each of them has helped me go through this painful and joyful transformation. Without them, the journey toward the birth of this book would have been impossible.

I give my deep appreciation to the faculty, students, and administrators of Riverside Junior and Senior High School for opening their doors to me, sharing their thoughts and information with me, and being tolerant of my presence in their rooms and my constant intrusive questions and interviews. Among the teachers, Jane, Susan, and Andy deserve special credit not only for letting me use their rooms as a base for my research but also for their contributions to data collection, for their establishing and maintaining links between me and their school, and for their valuable insights. I consider them my special partners in this research.

Among all the students and people who were involved in the study, I want particularly to thank Tran, Paw, Cham, and Sy and their family for opening themselves and their home to me. I know with their cultural background they had to have made double effort and have had great trust in me before they could open their hearts and home to a stranger. I thank them deeply for their trust in me and their tolerance of my constant, intrusive presence and endless questions. I owe them a great deal.

My special gratitude goes to my six former professors, who have contributed in unique ways to the construction of this study. Dr. Khleif's sharp criticism and strong discipline put me right on track. Dr. Sullivan's theoretical perspective helped me see what I was trying to say. For two years, with her unique listening pedagogy, Dr. Hansen allowed me to babble in the car on the way to our research base or in her office in order to search for words and ideas. Her constant nodding and quiet responses gave me confidence and direction. Dr. Schram was my cane throughout the drafting stages of this book. He was always available for whatever help I needed. He read drafts and drafts of my writing and gave his responses immediately and in detail. His most constructive input not only provided insight for my own study, but reassured me for what I had found and helped me see what I had missed.

Dr. Newkirk not only helped me clear my confusion and pushed me to another level of thinking in the research stage, but was responsible for the publication of this book. He read the book many times and gave suggestions for revision page by page. Without him, this book would have still sat on my shelf as a dissertation.

Dr. Graves directed this research. He was involved with every step of my study: finding funds, locating the research setting, contacting the proper personnel, data collecting, analyzing, and writing. Our long and constant conversations on the phone and over coffee and lunch for two years contributed to the construction of every piece of this study.

Many thanks go to my four very dear friends: Bonnie Sunstein, Peg Murray, Dan Seger, and Kay Morgan. Without their companionship, my long journey would have been unendurable, lonely, and difficult. The regular meetings and conversations with them stimulated my thinking, helped the organization of my thoughts, and sharpened my sensitivity.

Thanks also go to my three new friends and colleagues: Bess Altwerger, Karen Brown, and Barbara Kines. Like my old friends in New Hampshire, they continue to enlighten and support me in my new career. They helped and contributed to the revision of the book.

I am very grateful to the copyeditor and my production editor Joanne Tranchemontagne for the patience and effort that they put into the production of this book.

My family has sacrificed and contributed tremendously. Xiao-di grew up without a mother for three-and-a-half years and Fan adopted bachelorhood during that same time. Later they uprooted themselves to join me in this country, but still had to put up with having a mother and wife absent mentally. Having them near me gave me confidence and constant support. Credit should also be given to my father, for his leaving his comfortable home to come here to help me: stepping down from his authority position to help his daughter who, according to our cultural tradition, was supposed to kneel down and to serve him.

My deep appreciation goes to the Jarvis family: Edward, Yolanda, and Timothy. They are my extended family in this new land and have helped me and my family in whatever way they could. Yolanda, a former editor, spent hours and days editing my work. For a week, she simply moved into my place and worked on my book fulltime.

My last thanks goes to my American mother, Maryellen H. Mefford. She has made what I have become today possible. She provided me with the opportunity I couldn't have in my home country and gave me a home that I never felt I had. With her constant love, care, and support she has healed my wounds caused by being emotionally rejected at birth and being suppressed as a human being in my own country. In short, she has helped me to live a more human life, happier and freer than the one I was born to. She symbolizes America to me.

In summary, I thank America and its people for accepting me as one of them and providing me with a home where I felt comfortable. With their passionate love, warm support, and open minds and intelligence, they have liberated me as a person and educated me as a democratic educator.

 *Introduction*

Seven years ago, after I taught English at a college in China, I came to America to pursue a graduate degree. Before I left for America, many friends and colleagues who had been studying abroad warned me, "If you can, try not to major in English. It seems they don't read the same way as we do. You could never get it. It is their literature, we have no say about it." I did not understand what they meant, and I could not see giving up studying the Western literature I had loved since my childhood. Besides, what they said made me curious about the difference between Western and Chinese ways of reading.

As a preschooler, I listened to, and later read by myself, many Western fairy tales and children's stories, such as "Cinderella," "Little Red Riding Hood," "The Frog Prince," "The Match Girl," and "The Ugly Duckling." I was fascinated by the Western world, its culture, its ways of living, its customs, its ways of thinking, and its ways with words. The children's stories opened my mind to that far-away land, and I became interested in anything about the West. I wanted to know about that world more and more as I grew older. I never stopped reading, dreaming, and imagining about the people and life there.

When all the Chinese schools closed during the Cultural Revolution (1966–76), I was sent to work on a farm during my teenage years. Before leaving for the farm, I sneaked into the attic, where a dozen trunks full of books had been stored, sealed to "prevent poisoning the people with Western bourgeois ideology." I packed my suitcases with those "poisonous" books and left for the farm.

For four years on the farm, under the dim kerosene lamp, I educated myself with those books. They were translations of literature from Russia, Germany, France, Britain, and Spain. I read every night after working in the field or on rainy or snowy days, when I did not have to work. From those readings, I learned European history and geography; I was introduced to many different countries and cultures. Through those books, my mind traveled all over the world.

At the farm, I lived with four other girls my age. I shared my reading with them while we worked in the field or rested in our straw-roofed mud shed. They became more and more interested in my books and started to read on their own. We talked about our reading, and dreamed and imagined together what it would be like to live in the world we read about. Our little shed became a book club. Even many peasants came to listen to our stories. Once a peasant said to me, "Danling, if you die today, you won't regret, as you have known so much about the world." His words made me feel rich. The reading made those years of hard life more tolerable, enjoyable, and meaningful. Now, looking back at those years, I realize that was the time I read and enjoyed reading more than any other time in my life.

Years later, when I had a chance to go to college, I majored in English. I was so thrilled the first time I was able to read the original version of a book in English instead of the translation. From that time on I immersed myself in English and American literature. From Chaucer, Milton, and Shakespeare to Hawthorne, Melville, Dickinson, Hemingway, Steinbeck, Mark Twain, I learned the development of the British and American culture, language, history, and people. The learning of that world and its language inflamed my desire to see that world, experience that culture, and know the people there. I dreamed that some day I would read about that world with the people there.

In 1985, my lifelong dream came true when I was offered an opportunity to study in America. How, then, could I understand and accept the advice from many friends and colleagues that suggested I give up something I had loved my whole life? I still vividly remember what they said to me:

[Western literature] is something you can never get. It is their literature and culture. It is in their blood, and you can never understand or learn to read their works in their way. It is okay to study it here because we use our ways to interpret and understand it. Literature is the most difficult subject for people like us to learn in America, as we didn't grow up there. Don't try to get any degrees in the field of literature in America. It will kill you no matter how hard you try. Just imagine if any foreigners could understand our classics like *The Dreams of the Red Chamber* as we do. It is impossible for them, just as the study of their literature is impossible for us. That is why you can hardly see any Oriental faces in the liberal arts field, even few American Chinese. Westerners read differently from us; we can never get it. Majoring in anything for us is easier than literature in America.

Their words were very persuasive, but taking their advice was out of the question for me at that time. Western literature had given me the most joy and meaning in my life so far. I had wanted to learn how the Western people interpreted their world and words through their literature. I wanted to find out the difference between my way of interpreting their world and theirs. I wanted to be able to enjoy their literature in as much depth as I did my Chinese literature. When I was reading foreign literature, there were always some hints, some nuances, some implications or words between the lines that I would miss. I wanted to study the literature in its native land so the people there would help me to understand things that I had no way to learn in China.

The Master's Program in English

As soon as I arrived in America, I applied to study in an English master's program in a college. Before I started my English courses, my mind was filled with joy and excitement when I pictured myself sitting among all Americans discussing their literature, their world, and their culture. I was sure I was going to get the most authentic interpretation of American literature!

Before I went to a class, I would always carefully read the assignment, twice at least. But when the discussion began, it was as if I had read a different book from everyone else in the class. I expected we would discuss our interpretations of the text, how the author tried to tell us about his or her world and time, and how the writing reflected his or her ways of understanding the world and the time. But in almost every literature course, the discussion would focus more on the art of composing rather than the meaning of a text. We concentrated on such things as symbolism, Romanticism, imagery, literature elements—such as plot, setting, point of view, characters—the structure of a text, and the language and tone of a text. Characters were not analyzed as people, and a setting was not looked at as a place. They were seen simply as elements of the text structure. A text was discussed as if it had nothing to do with the real world and people. With this way of reading the text, it seemed that the author did not mean to write to express him/herself or intend to tell the readers something through the writing, but only to show how he or she could manipulate words and language. I could not understand why the art of composing was so over-stressed at the expense of the meaning of the text. How could I be interested in the structure of a text before its content made sense to me?

I became more and more lost and confused in my classes. It seemed I was too far behind my peers. I had many questions that concerned the meaning of the text, and I wished that the class discussion would help me solve those problems. But the class always jumped into the discussion of some kind of ism at the very first minute. Then I became too confused or over-whelmed to ask, or even remember, any of my questions. Very often I left the class feeling humiliated and frustrated. I did not think I knew anything or could even read. Once I told one of my classmates about my frustration and asked how I could learn to read like they did. He took me to the library, point-ing at the reference books and said to me, "Those books will help you, especially those Cliff's Notes."

The reference books and Cliff's Notes were saviors. I spent more time reading them than the assignment itself before I went to class. I learned to rely heavily on them for every writing assignment. I tried to imitate the right tone and adopt the Western ways of reading. But the more I became dependent on the reference books and critics' work for my reading and writing, the more I felt I could not read and write. I did not think I had any background to study literature and blamed my Chinese professors for not teaching me this way to read and write in China.

However, no matter how hard I tried to learn the "proper" ways to read and write about literature, I continued to suffer feelings of loss and confusion. One day we read a poem that ended with some lines about waves splashing on the rocks on the shore. I liked this image a lot. To me, it portrayed the power and the beauty of nature: when shapeless and colorless waves formed together moving toward the same destination, they created shape, color, strength, and sound. They symbolized solidarity and determination. But when I went to the class, I was shocked by how some of my American peers looked at this image. They saw it as sexual: a hard rock surrounded by foam created by the striking of waves on the rock. I became speechless by the world of difference between the way my peers and I interpreted this image. When I found no one had reacted to the poem as I had, I felt so left out. I never thought literature would be a world so unfamiliar, remote, and strange to me. I wondered, "Do all Americans read and talk about literature like this?"

I became more and more silent and felt more and more alienated in classes as the semesters went by. I stopped thinking about or trying to understand the others. I lost interest in reading and felt burdened by all the writing assignments. I had a knot in my stomach every time I went to class. I wished I would have taken my Chinese friends' advice and not gotten myself into this mess. As a successful student in China, I used to enjoy challenge in my learning, but as a graduate student in America, I felt helpless, incapable, and defeated, as if I were lost in a strange jungle.

I had expected that the study of American literature would help me not only understand the English language better, but also, more important, understand the American people, culture, and world. For instance, when I read *The Adventures of Huckleberry Finn*, I wanted to learn in what way the character Finn represented American youngsters at the time, what American values Mark Twain conveyed through the characterization of Finn, how American people identified themselves with Finn and any other characters in the story, and how black Americans interpreted Mark Twain's characterization of Jim. But when we studied this book in class, the discussion was either on the possible homosexual relationship between Huck and Jim, or on the black dialect used in the writing. The discussion, which connected so little with the real world and real people, did not help me understand the story much. Instead, it left me feeling more confused about this world and more remote toward its people.

I took many courses and studied various genres—drama, poetry, novels, and short stories. But I can hardly remember what I read, and I have even forgotten most of the titles and authors. But I remember very well the books I read when I was a child or on the farm twenty or thirty years ago. When I talk about those books I still feel warmth and joy. I can even recite some of the lines and quotations from those books I read years ago.

When I received my master's degree upon graduation, instead of feeling a sense of accomplishment or pride, I felt relieved and disabled. But I refused to end my journey this way and live with a defeated feeling for the rest of my life. I decided to continue for a doctorate. I switched my field from English to education, as I was fearful of continuing to suffer the alienation for four more years. I applied to the Reading and Writing Instruction program at the University of New Hampshire.

The Reading and Writing Instruction Program

After my first meeting with my new professors and peers, I felt like Alice in Wonderland. This program was formed by a community of fine writers. Among my peers were poets, fiction writers, published authors, and even a former president of the National Writing Center Association. I was an ESL student and a newcomer to the culture who was still struggling to understand others and express myself in English. I thought I must have been accepted into this program by mistake. From the close and lively interaction between the peers and professors, I could tell there would be no way for me to hide and remain silent all the way through, as I had done in the master's English program. Soon, I was sure, my ignorance as a reader and writer in this Western world would be found out. Then I would be deported, with a typically polite Western apology given in a firm tone. Nervously, I started the program.

At my first reading class, I was prepared to hear books discussed with a "formalist" view or "decontructionist" bent, or to hear talk of sexual images and symbolism. I was surprised when the professor started the class by reading a story and invited the students to share our connections with the story or our identification with the characters. Instead of giving us reading assignments, she asked us to make our own reading list. In the class, we read, talked, and wrote, not like English majors, but as real people did in life. For the first time in so long, I left the class with a kind of joyful satisfaction.

During subsequent reading discussions in this class, we shared our understanding and feelings about the reading. We made the connection between the world in the text and real life; we identified with the characters and experiences portrayed in the novels. We also questioned and argued with the authors and texts. In short, we reacted to the reading with feelings and emotions, we used everyday language rather than a special discourse, we discussed the meaning of the text as well as the ways the meaning was constructed. Not only could I understand everyone in the class, but I identified with their connections and thoughts. I felt I was not an outsider, but a reader like anyone else in the class. Instead of being silent and hiding in the corner, I joined in class discussions and many times voluntarily shared my response to the reading.

I went to my first writing class also with nervousness, as I was not sure what kind of tone and language I would have to borrow to get through it. In my earlier literature courses, I had Cliff's Notes. For this course I might have to find new aids. Writing like a doctorate student, I assumed, I might have to sound like Marx or Dewey. To my surprise, the professor started the class by asking us each to tell a story, a childhood story. He told his own story first, with a personal, intimate, and nostalgic tone. One by one we told ours. I never thought I had a story to tell, but I was intrigued by the others' stories. They reminded me of my childhood, my life on the farm and my experiences growing up in unheated cement apartment buildings in China. I told my story:

> In China, in the area where I lived, we didn't have fireplace like you have here with chimney on the roof. We don't have central heat neither. When it was cold, we just put more clothes on. In winter, we dressed a lot no matter when we were outside or inside the house. We dressed our children with so much that they could barely walk. So they fell all the time. But as they were bundled with so much clothes on, when they fell down, they never hurt themselves, as their noses were at least two inches above from the ground. Of course they had hard time to get up too. When I was on the farm, in very very cold days, each farmer would contribute a bundle of woods and get together in our little hut. They lit fire in the middle of our mud and straw-roof house, like American Indians did in the woods. All the peasants in the village would all come, chatting, smoking, and making fun of each other around the fire. Sometimes we would kill a dog and eat it around the fire. We believe dog meat gives you most heat. That was the best time of the year.

The sharing of our memories and stories connected us and set an intimate tone for the class. We shared, laughed, and learned about each other. My peers showed great interest in my story, as it was so different from the others'. They kept asking me questions, and I kept talking and talking. I probably said more in that one time than in two years in the master's English program. We wrote a lot in that class. In our writing, we told about our own experiences, discussed the things that interested or bothered us, and shared our observation and understanding of the world and life.

I was a different writer in the Reading and Writing program than I had been in the English program. In the latter, I tried hard to sound like an English major in my writing. I imitated how the critics read and analyzed the text. Not only did I adopt their ways of reading a text, but I also borrowed their terms and tone to discuss a text. A paragraph from one of my English papers, a discussion of Willy Loman, one of the main characters in Arthur Miller's *Death of a Salesman*, is typical:

> Willy's situation exactly reflects this timeless universal problem. The sense of his modernness, I assume, is that his world is a modern one, so he has to wear modern clothes and display what is the most modern. Otherwise his tragedy can hardly bring about any pleasure of terror, pity, and thought on the part of the modern audience. In essence, his dilemma is not different from Oedipus' and Hamlet's, and may actually be even worse in our modern world because man is more devalued than he was in Greek and Elizabethan ages.

Writing in the UNH program was different. The essential thing was to be yourself. Instead of relying heavily on outside references, I had to go deep inside myself, to find what I knew and who I was. Instead of sounding like someone else, I had to sound like me. It was not easy at first. After two years of training in the English program, I thought I had finally learned to sound like an English major, able to use academic discourse and a Western intellectual tone. Now I had to twist back to myself again. I did not know my own thoughts any more after giving them no value for two years. In expressing this feeling, I wrote:

> My maternal grandmother told me that it was excruciatingly painful when she had to relearn to walk with her unbound feet after they had been bound for months. At present, I am in a similar situation to my grandmother's in learning to write with

my voice. After I have been trained to sound like somebody else for years in writing, I don't know my voice any more. It is like a faded memory, so distant, so strange, and so vague. Did I have a voice of my own? Can I have it back? Am I deformed as a writer?

For a while I struggled. Slowly my numb mind started to wake up, and I gained consciousness by constant writing and sharing of my own experiences, my own feelings, and my own understanding of the things and people around me. I wrote not only academic papers, but also poems and stories, which surprised me, as I rarely wrote any stories and poems even in my native language after I entered college. Here is one of the first poems I tried in English:

A Woman Without a Name

My grandma never had a name.
When she was little,
She was called Daughter Number One.
When she was married,
She became Mrs. So and So.
After she had children,
People called her the mother of the Zhangs' house.

My grandma always wanted a name.
Once, she shook her mother's knees begging her:
"Mom, would you please give me a name?"
Slowly moving her head from her sewing, with a deep sigh,
Her mother answered her:
"Honey, I wish I could,
But girls are not supposed to have names."

My grandma always loved roses,
Especially, those red ones.
One night, her mom whispered into her ear
While she was asleep:
"Red Rose, oh, I wish I could call you,
My little Red Rose."
"Red Rose, oh, I would love that name,"
My grandma exclaimed with joy and regret,

When she heard what her mother called her
While she was asleep.

Red Rose, a name, my grandma always wanted,
But she was only called once by that name
In her sleep.

She lived for seventy-one years without a name.
At her tomb, we carved:

Red Rose Chang
1880–1951

Compared to those of my peers, my poems and stories sounded much more raw and childish; but writing them helped me discover something in me, and also helped me to understand risk-taking in learning and explore other ways to express myself.

I read and wrote all the time. Because I no longer had to pretend or act like someone else, the reading and writing became easy, even a joy, for me. I could not stop. I did not read and write just for assignments, for grades, or for professors, but for myself. I found I had so much to say and express, and I had little difficulty expressing myself in English. It was as if I had gone back to my farm life—no constraints, no deadlines, no requirements. I simply immersed myself in reading and writing. By the end of the first semester, I had read thirty-two books, twice as many as what I had read in two years in the English program. I had written over two hundred pieces in addition to a dozen research papers for the courses I took, more than I had ever written in the thirteen years since I first learned English.

In this learning community, people constantly shared their reading, writing, and thinking in classes, at research meetings, at almost any gathering. At first I was not used to this interaction and openness in learning. Overwhelmed and confused by so much unfamiliarity, I sat silently through many classes and research meetings. My professors and peers did not leave me alone for too long, though. They poked me with all kinds of questions, starting with those about China, then moving to America. I spoke first in a whispering voice and timid tone: many people had to lean forward in order to hear me. Gradually, with the encouragement of their interest and curiosity in whatever I said, my voice became louder and louder.

Instead of sitting there and feeling stupid, overwhelmed and confused with what I did not know, I began to ask questions of my own: from "What is 'lunch duty'?" and "What is 'basal'?" to "Why do you Americans have to worry about how students are evaluated? In China, evaluation is the work of the authorities. We teachers simply teach, we even have no say about what textbooks we have to teach" and "What's the relationship between students' self-evaluation and teaching?"

No matter what kind of questions I asked, I never got the slightest hint that my classmates were looking down on me as a person too ignorant to be one of them (something I was very much afraid of). My peers and professors never thought my questions were too trivial or naive. They always answered my questions patiently, discussed them with me enthusiastically, and generally showed great interest in my questions and ideas. They were often fascinated by the way I phrased and expressed my ideas. They were seldom bothered by my accent, nonstandard English expressions, and different metaphors and images. Instead, they were amused by them and interpreted them as unique, reflecting a sort of Oriental beauty and a different perspective. I was surprised by their recognition of something in me that I had never valued and sometimes even felt ashamed of.

This recognition invited me into the literate community that I had felt no part of at the beginning, built my confidence as a learner, and overcame both my fear and my feeling of being an outsider. Through constant sharing and discussion about reading, writing, and many issues of education and literacy with my peers and mentors, I understood more and more about American society, culture, and people. In turn, this understanding helped me look at my native culture and world with a different perspective. My learning about the two worlds enlightened me and made me a reader, a writer, and a thinker with a much broader viewpoint. I was eager to express myself. My timid, uncertain, soft voice became strong and passionate. In the past, when I had tried hard to sound like others in my reading and writing, I alienated both myself and others. Now that I could just be myself as a reader and writer, I came to know myself more and more, became closer to the people around me, and joined the community from which I had feared I would always be excluded in this Western world. I grew as a writer who integrated Oriental and Western styles and a thinker whose views combined Marxism and pragmatism. Rather than hindering my new learning and research, my Chinese cultural and formal academic training and background became strengths.

The Teaching of Reading and Writing

My two very different learning experiences as a newcomer to America helped me understand the teaching of reading and writing. My earlier experience alienated me as a learner; the later one liberated me. My growing experiences as a literate person in the Reading and Writing Instruction program made me realize that I was a reader and writer who was different in many ways from many people in this culture. When I had difficulty understanding the others, or reading and thinking like my peers, it was not because of my low English language ability or my lack of knowledge of the Western world, but because of my different ways of reading the words and the world and my different ways of expressing myself. Once I realized the beauty in my difference instead of denying myself and feeling inferior, I found my voice in reading and writing. I had the language and fluency to express myself in book discussion and writing. I could think, read, and write with power and imagination.

I know there are many students in America who had or are having the same learning experiences as I had when I was in the master's English program. They doubted or are still doubting their ability as readers and writers in this new culture. Many of them might be still struggling in their school and trying hard to adapt themselves to the school's ways of learning. Many of them might have already given up their study or switched to something they thought demanded less reading and writing. America is a multiracial and multicultural society. Not only are my experiences shared by those who have recently come to this country; they are also shared by many others who simply have different social, cultural, and language backgrounds than the one that dominates the school's ways of learning. Seeing so few minority students in the field of liberal arts and so many students struggling in this country, I realize I may be one of the few who have survived, and survived long enough in this field to regain joy, confidence, and interest in reading and writing. Many people may have given up learning before they ever experienced any joy and excitement as readers and writers.

As an educator, I want to help those students who are suffering the same humiliation, frustration, and alienation in their reading and writing as I did when I first came to study in America. I want to help teachers in this country understand these students. I want to show that once reading and writing connect with students' backgrounds and experiences, everyone can read and write. It is not that some of our students are unable to learn; it is our teaching approach that sometimes fails to reach them, to discover their potential as learners, to invite them into our learning community.

That is why I have written this book. I focus on students who, for various reasons, are marginalized at school. I want to find out how school learning can help students who have recently come to this country become literate persons in their new culture, make connections with others, and generally learn how to live in their new world. Maybe subconsciously I want to relive my old learning experiences through the study of people like me, and retake the journey, which at the time I was too confused and overwhelmed to understand and enjoy.

I want this book to contribute to our understanding of a diverse student population, and of reading and writing instruction.

My study focuses on four Laotian refugee adolescents' learning experiences in an American secondary school. All four are siblings, the youngest of nine children of the Savang family. They came to the United States two years ago from a Thai refugee camp.

Tran (age 19), Cham (age 17), Paw (age 16), and Sy (age 14) are students in Riverside Junior and Senior High School. The three oldest are in the eleventh grade; Sy is in the seventh grade. They spend most of the day in the mainstream classes, and one or two hours in the ESL (English as a Second Language) room each day for special help with their English.

Riverside Junior and Senior High School is located in a typical New England small town. Until the 1980s, the population was 99 percent middle-class Caucasian; in the late 1980s, large numbers of Southeast Asian immigrants moved into the town. Now, of the 401 students in the school, 365 (91 percent) are white, 26 (6.5 percent) are Laotian, and 10 (2.5 percent) are other minorities (black, Mexican, Korean, Chinese, Japanese, and Philippine).

Two part-time ESL tutors, Jane and Andy, work daily in the school with the ten students who need the ESL service. Among these ten students, nine are Laotian, who have been in the United States between two and five years, and one is Mexican, who arrived just a few months ago. Jane works until 12:30 P.M.; Andy leaves for another job around 11:30 A.M. Neither Jane nor Andy has any training in ESL teaching. Jane deals mainly with English reading and writing, and Andy usually helps students with their science and math. They have separate rooms. Jane's room is at the end of a hall; she has one table by a window. Andy's room is only as big as two ping-pong tables; at most it can accommodate three students plus himself. The two tutors have students come to them at different periods all the time they are at school. Besides helping students with their classroom work and language practice, Jane and Andy serve as the students' liaison at school and consultants on life in the new culture. All the students love to come to their ESL rooms, as if these were their homes at school. There they are often heard talking, laughing, joking, and sometimes teasing each other. While I was a participant-researcher at Riverside, I also served as a third ESL tutor. As I got to know the children better, I became their friend, driving them around, helping them at home, and joining and also inviting them to parties and social gatherings.

The reason I chose Tran, Cham, Paw, and Sy as my case studies is that they had recently come to this country and so had more cultural and linguistic adjustments to make. Also, they were from the same family. Having all four from the same family I thought would reduce research costs, and would also help me see them not simply as Laotians but as four individuals.

This book contains six chapters and a conclusion. Chapter 1 provides background on the four siblings: their family and life in their home country, in their refugee camps, and in the United States. Chapter 2 describes the four adolescents and their general situation at school. Chapters 3 through 6 are case studies of the four—one chapter each for Tran, Paw, Cham, and Sy—with a focus on their reading and writing experiences at school. The case studies are organized thematically rather than chronologically (according to their ages). Chapters 3 and 4, on Tran and Paw, describe what kind of readers and writers they are naturally and what kind of readers and writers they are taught to be at school. Chapters 5 and 6, on Cham and Sy, show what kind of readers and writers they are when teaching matches or mismatches their learning patterns. In the Conclusion, I reflect on the study and discuss issues related to literacy instruction and multiculturalism in the field of education.

Chapter One

The Story of the Savang Family

*T*he story of the Savang family reveals the past experiences, the feelings, the dreams, and the life in the new culture of the family generally, and Tran, Cham, Paw, and Sy in particular. Knowledge of their past history and their present life will help us understand and interpret their behavior at school. It reveals why they had to leave their own country, how much they gave up for their present pursuits, and what kind of adjustments they have had to make in their new life. Furthermore, learning the details of their story will help us see other dimensions of Tran, Cham, Paw, and Sy so that we can look at them as four individuals instead of just four Laotians.

The Savangs' story also suggests an important aspect of the connective ways of learning: learning language and learning to read and write should be connected to the learner's life experiences and personal interests. These four youngsters have many stories to tell, but they have few chances to tell their stories in their school experiences. As a result, they remain strange to others and sometimes even to themselves.

The Savang family came from Laos, a country in Southeast Asia about the size of the state of Oregon. Laos, a landlocked country, is bordered by China on the north, Cambodia on the south, Thailand and Burma on the west, and Vietnam on the east. The economy of Laos is based largely on agriculture, rice being the most important product. There are no railroads, and some of the highways are unusable several months of the year. The Mekong River is the main waterway for transportation. The lack of transportation and communication limits the economic development of the country.

Since the end of the eighteenth century, Laos was ruled mainly by Thailand and France, though it was also for a short time under the control of Japan during World War II. In 1954, it achieved full independence from France. During the Vietnam War, it became a base for the U.S. army. The Laotian army and air force were trained and sponsored by the United States. Laotian soldiers and civilians fought with the Americans during the Vietnam War. In order to destroy the Ho Chi Minh trail and cut off the back roads of the North Vietnamese army, U.S. fighters dropped bombs in Laos every day. Three times more bombs were dropped in Laos than in Vietnam. During those years, the Laotian people, especially those in the northeast areas (mainly Hmongs), could not live a normal life and had no peace. Many Laotian refugee children remember nothing of their country but wars and bombs.

In 1975, Laotian Communists took over control of the country. They punished those who used to work for the Americans and for the old government. They also took land and businesses away from the owners. Since then people have constantly tried to escape from Communist control and punishment. The current exodus of refugees from Laos began at that time. The Savang family was among those refugees.

The Savang family has nine children, four girls and five boys. The first year in their life that Tran, Cham, Paw, and Sy remember living together as a family is 1990. From 1975, when the Communists took over the country, until 1990, their family had been fragmented (see Table 1–1). They moved from Laos to Thailand, to the Philippines, and lastly to the United States. Once in the United States, they moved from house to house until they bought their own.

The Savangs had been a well-to-do family in Laos. The children's great-grandfather was an army officer, "some kind of chief commander," Tran told me. He is still alive, in his nineties, in Laos. The grandfather was a businessman who "owned all the fur business in Lao." He made a lot of money

Year(s)	Location	Living Situation
1975–83	Communist Laos	Father in a reeducation camp. Mother at home with three children (Paw and Sy with mother). Six children living with different families (Tran and Cham at two different uncles' houses).
		1983–87: The family escaped from Laos to Thai refugee camps in twos or threes.
1987–88	Thai refugee camps	Father and mother with one daughter in one camp. Eight children in another camp.
1988–89	Massachusetts, USA	Parents with five children in one apartment. Two older sisters staying with sponsor. Tran and Cham in an uncle's house.
1989–90	Riverside, NH	Parents with three children in a small apartment. Paw and Sy staying in a friend's home on Woodland Drive. Tran, Cham, and two sisters staying in Massachusetts.
1990–91	Riverside, NH	Parents and seven children in a duplex apartment. Two older sisters renting an apartment in Massachusetts.
1991–	Riverside, NH	Parents and seven children in their own home. Two older sisters visit on weekends.

Table 1–1 The locations and living situation of the Savang family

trading with the Europeans. "He was so rich, and had so much money. Every night he and my grandmother would count the money, bind the bills together, and sleep on them." He built three houses, one for European businessmen to stay in. Later, he became very sick. He died before the Communists came.

Mr. Savang, the father of the family, was a pilot who had trained in the United States in the late 1960s. Later he became a pilot instructor in the Laotian air force. The Laotian air force was sponsored by the United States, so Mr. Savang in essence worked for the Americans. Mrs. Savang, the mother, owned a clothing store and sold her goods mainly in the open market. When the Communists took over the country in 1975, Mr. Savang was sent to a reeducation camp with others who had worked for the old government and the Americans. He stayed in the camp for twelve years and was made to work very hard there. "After I worked there for those years, there will be no hardship I can't handle any more." That was all he told his children about his years in the camp.

During those twelve years in the camp, Mr. Savang was never allowed to come home, and Mrs. Savang went there to visit him only twice. After the father was taken away, the nine children had to live with different families. They moved to the uncles' and aunts'. Tran and Cham went to live with two different uncles' families in different towns. Paw stayed with her mother, as she was too young to go anywhere else. Sy was born after his father was taken away. Sy met his father for the first time when he was almost eleven.

All the children went to school in Laos. According to what they said in public (that is, what they told the school; some of them told me different stories), Tran had seven years of schooling in Laos, Cham had five years, Paw had three years, and Sy had one year. Tran was the only one of the four children who could read and write in Lao.

The family was Buddhist. All the Savang boys except Sy had been monks in Laos for a certain period of time in their lives. That was the Lao Buddhist tradition: boys had to be monks for a certain time in their lives in order to grow up. Tran became a monk twice, once when he was five and later at the age of seven. Each time he lived in the temple for several months. Cham was a monk for about a week at the age of seven. As monks, they had to shave their heads, get up between four and five o'clock in the morning to study Buddhist scripture, and learn to discipline themselves.

Between 1983 and 1987, the family managed to escape to Thai refugee camps. They escaped separately. Two older daughters made it out first. After they were settled in a camp, the two older sons joined them. Six months later, Cham and Paw escaped with some other relatives and found their sisters and brothers at the camp. Tran and Sy joined a group of escapees who had paid for people to take them out of Laos. When Mr. Savang was released from the reeducation camp in 1987, he left Laos with his wife and a daughter. They were the last group of the family to escape. It took three years and ten months for the whole family to get out of Laos. They were lucky: all of them survived. This was rare for refugee families.

In the Thai refugee camps, the Savang family was not together. Mr. and Mrs. Savang and the daughter who had left Laos with them stayed in one camp, and the rest of the children stayed at a different one. The two camps were miles apart. The camps contained buildings with large halls. Each family had to buy boards to separate the halls into smaller rooms. Each family had one room. They slept on the floor and cooked in the room. Cooking in the rooms resulted in many fire accidents. Whoever caused the fire would be sent to the camp jail for one or two years as punishment.

There was no electricity and no water. People had to walk about a mile to get water and wash themselves in a lake. As a result, many people did not bother to wash themselves for months, and many became sick. Long lines of patients would wait outside the camp clinics to be treated. People died every day.

The camps were fenced with iron wires. The refugees were not allowed to leave without permission. If they did, they would be put into the camp jail for several months to a year, or be fined if they could afford to pay. The food, mainly rice and canned vegetables, was rationed. The canned vegetables were sent by the United Nations; the rice had bugs. Those with money could buy some food and vegetables from the local people who brought things to the camps to sell, but these goods were expensive.

Each camp had its own office, which hired refugees. Those who had jobs at the camp could get more food for their families. The Savangs' two older daughters had jobs in the camp, so they were able to get the family more food. Still, it was not enough. Very often the boys would sneak out to catch some fish in the lake. Cham did this most frequently. If they were caught, they would be in trouble. The father also had a job in his camp. He was a translator for the refugees and the English-speaking camp service people. He often stayed in hotels with the camp service workers.

The camps had police who were all Thai soldiers. As the Savang children told me, "Those soldiers were very mean to us refugees. They took money away from us, and yelled and punished us for no reasons. They hated us because we caused troubles for their country."

The refugee camps had schools too. The children went to school a couple of hours a day to learn English. The teachers were Laotians, Thais, and Americans. There must have been some Christian church services there as well, because the children said that they went to Sunday school and studied the Bible. "That was how we became Christian in the camp," Cham and Paw told me.

The refugees had to wait at the camps until they were sponsored by the people in the country they would go to. The Savang family stayed in the camps for three years before they got a sponsor from America. Once they had a sponsor, but before coming to the United States, the family stayed in the Philippines for seven months, in Tran's words, "to learn how to live in America." Finally, in 1988, the whole family arrived in the United States. First they settled in a town in Massachusetts, where their sponsor's family was located. A year later, the Savangs moved to Riverside, because of job opportunities.

For the first couple of years in the United States, the Savang family could not live together due to the small places they could afford to rent. Two older daughters lived with the sponsor's family. Tran and Cham stayed with an uncle's family in Massachusetts. When the family moved to Riverside, those four children did not come with the rest of the family. They stayed where they were until a year later, when the family moved into a bigger apartment.

In recent years, because a seafood plant is located in a nearby city, many Laotians moved into the town of Riverside, New Hampshire. Most of them, about forty Laotian families, lived on Woodland Drive, in an apartment complex with no lawns and few trees. The simple ranch-style apartments are exactly the same size and color. Each has two small bedrooms, a tiny living room, a bathroom, and a kitchen. It was originally built for the students of a nearby college until the Laotian community found this affordable place for themselves. All the apartments were connected into a long, flat building, shaped in a half circle with a parking lot in the middle. Each family parked their car right in front of their apartment door. The community set up a basketball backboard and a volleyball net at the side of the parking lot, which also served as a playground for the children. During some special occasions, the parking lot would become a place for community gatherings.

When the Savangs first came to Riverside, they did not move into Woodland Drive, as the apartments were too small for their family. They rented an apartment not far away from Woodland Drive, but it was not big enough for their family either. They had to send their two youngest children, Paw and Sy, to live with a friend's family on Woodland Drive for a couple of months until they found a bigger place. In 1990, the family moved into an apartment in a duplex, and all the children except the two older daughters moved back in from other people's houses. For the first time since 1975, the family was together and settled as a family.

Though the Savang family did not live on Woodland Drive, they had a very close relationship with the community. Whenever there were gatherings for holiday celebrations and weddings, the Savangs would be there. Mr. Savang's former pilot colleagues lived there, so he would often go there to visit them or invite them to his house for drinks and a chat during the holidays and on weekends. Most of the women there were Mrs. Savang's fellow workers in the seafood factory. Woodland was the only place in town where she could visit friends. The Savang children sometimes went to play sports with the children there. For them, that was the only social place besides school. The Savangs knew everybody and everything happening on Woodland Drive, and would participate in any activities held by the Laotian community.

Like most of the other Laotian people on Woodland Drive, the Savang family members had either factory or low-skill jobs. Mr. Savang and two older sons worked on an assembly line from 7 A.M. to 7 P.M. in a medical technology factory in a nearby town. The mother and one daughter worked on the assembly line from 3 P.M. to midnight in a seafood factory, twelve miles away from where they lived. They all would work overtime whenever they could. The two older daughters, who lived away, worked as nurse's aides in a hospital and also as house helpers for the sponsor's family, as the wife was bedridden.

In March 1991, the Savangs bought a big house in Riverside with the three-year accumulated savings of seven family members. The house was beautiful, with four bedrooms and four acres of land. The four children still in school also tried to work to help buy the house. Tran and Cham worked at the seafood factory after school for a few weeks; Paw went house to house selling cosmetics, besides cooking for the family every day after school. Sy was too young to work. He said that he would try to get a job the next summer. The father let the children keep half of their earnings; the other half went to the family.

Mr. Savang told me that everybody in his house tried very hard to keep the family going in their new land. When they left their homeland, they left everything behind except what they wore. But they had a dream, a beautiful dream: to search for a better life in America. That helped them endure losing whatever they had: their land, their houses, their people, and their culture—everything they were familiar with. They believed that they could start a new life, a beautiful new life in America—their dream land. But when they got here, they found there were so many things they had to adjust to. They even had to adjust to each other as a family.

For the first time since they could remember, Tran, Cham, Paw, and Sy have their parents and almost all their siblings together. It is not easy for them. Though they work very hard to keep the family together, each has his or her complaints.

Paw says:

I don't like my father. He is mean to us, never smiles, always has a stone face. I never talk to him unless I have to. He never talks to us either. I am comfortable with old people or small children, and nervous with others. Sometimes my father yelled at me, I just want to leave. But I am afraid to hurt my mother. My mother said my father changed. He was not like this before he went to reeducation camp. He is brainwashed. But I don't know what he was before. He left home when I was only a baby. I don't like Cham either. He is just like my father, so self-centered.

Cham says:

I don't like anybody in my house. I can't get along with any one of them. I don't know, I don't know why, I just don't like anybody.

Tran says:

I don't like my mother. I don't know them. I never live with them before. I want to move. I am not used to having so many people in the house. It is too messy. You don't have any minute of yourself. You can't do anything. When you want to read, they walk in and watch TV. My mother yells at me all the time. I have my way to do things, step by step, but she just wants me

25

to do things in her way. I can't get along with Cham. He is just like my mom, always thinks of money and wants to make money. I want to go to live with my sisters, to go back to my old school, I like there better. But I don't know, I'll have to see.

Sy, the youngest, says:

My parents never talk to me, never discuss about my future. I am too young. They don't talk to me. Sometimes they talk to my brothers and sisters, but not me. They all can discipline me, but I can't do anything to them. They are older, can do anything to me. They said I don't know anything. Yes, I don't know anything. I am too young.

The four school-age children seldom see other members of their family except on the weekends. Every day when they come home, their parents and older siblings are at work. In addition to the fact that the family does not have much time to talk to each other, spending time just for conversation is not in their tradition. They each know the rules of the house and their own responsibilities to the family. As Mr. Savang said, "I told my children to obey their parents, to respect the old people, to help each other. That is our tradition."

Every day after school, Paw cooks dinner for the family. The boys take turns doing the dishes and cleaning the house. No bargains. Everybody has to share the housework if he or she is home. For the school-age children, school and housework are the major things they do every day. They do not have much social life and have few friends.

From what they told me, I understand that they miss their life in Laos a lot. What they remember the most is what they cannot have at the present. They have recently come to a new culture and cannot figure it out, and yet they can no longer live as they used to. It is as if they have stopped at a crossroad: they cannot go back to where they came from and do not know which way to take to move on; they're just standing there, puzzled and confused.

Tran is a social person. He likes to make friends, to talk, to discuss world affairs and national events. But in this new culture, he has few chances to share his thinking. He feels lonely and out of control of his life here:

> I was a kind of student leader in Lao school. I had a lot of friends and we did a lot of fun things together. In Laos, we not only learned things from books, but also learned how to help people and the country. We did a lot of good things for the people and the country. That was fun.
>
> But here nothing is certain. I can't say what I want to do or what I want to be. I don't know what kind of life I want to have. Everything depends on my English. When my English gets good, I can do more things.

Cham is fascinated by all the shining, noisy, and fast-moving things in the new culture. He wants to try everything: parties, skating, skiing, bowling, games, swimming, and trips. He will go with anybody if he can try new things. He watches commercials on TV, reads ads in newspapers and magazines. That is how he learns about his new culture. But he has found he cannot afford to do what he wants. He misses what he could do in his home country.

> In Laos, I had a lot of friends. We played with the kids all the time. We played soccer, kites, fishing, hunting, and played marbles. But here no matter what you do, you have to have money. In Laos, we made our own stuff to play. We made kites with bamboo and paper, made sprint shot with the branches from the trees. We hunted birds with it. We made fish post with some sticks. We played marbles with our fingers. Here you don't make things. You buy things to play. You go to the mall to spend money playing. Here you have to have money to have friends. In Laos, we didn't have to. I want to make money, then I can try things. Here they have so many rules that we don't know. You can't fish here and hunt there, so we don't know what we should do.

Paw is a family-oriented person. What she misses most is her great-grandma. She does not care much about social life, but she wants a person whom she can trust and be close to.

She wants to try new things in the new culture, but she does not want to give up her past.

> I missed my grandma and my hometown most. She couldn't come with us. She didn't want to come. I was most close to her. We talked all the time. She taught me a lot of things. Before I left, she asked me whether I would continue to be a Buddhist. Yes, I told her I would always be a Buddhist no matter what. Now I am a Buddhist and a Christian. I have double religion. Now she is dead, died a year ago. I am used to the life here now. It was very difficult for me when we first came.

Sy does not remember much of his life in Laos, because he left the country at such a young age. He has a vague memory of the house where he used to live. But there are one or two things he can never forget. He likes to talk about his refugee camp life. He misses the friends he made there and the things he did with them that he cannot do with the kids here.

> I never can forget the New Year's celebration in my home town. We stood at the top of the temple, looking down. There was the Prince's castle beside the temple and by the lake. It was so beautiful. You could see the reflections of the temple and castle down the lake. Wow, I can never forget that. I miss going to the temple with my mother, and miss the New Year celebration with lots of people and games everywhere.
>
> I remember my life in the refugee camp. We played with many friends there. Once I made a kite, like this [*he draws a kite shaped as a butterfly*]. It flew so high, very high. I was so happy. Here you can't make it, because there is no bamboo. Kids here don't make things to play, they buy things to play. They spent money to play.

All the members of the Savang family miss their past. Mr. Savang misses the country and his profession; Mrs. Savang misses her houses and her business; the older sons and daughters feel their life is less meaningful here than in Laos. Mr. Savang says:

> I miss my country and flying. I still want to do something with airplanes. I know I have to go to school to have more educa-

28

tion. But I have a family to support, so I can't afford to go to school. Some day I wish I could.

Tran says about his mother:

My mother misses our houses in Laos a lot. That is why she wants to buy our own house so much. She misses her clothes store there too. That's why she still helps my uncle to sell things from his store. She loves to do business. Some day she wants to have her own business in this country.

The second oldest son says:

In Laos, we might be doctors, engineers, or pilots. We would go to college. But we can't do that here. Now what we do is just a job, not we like it or not, just do it for living. Here we don't have many friends, work and go home, that's what we do every day. Here we simply survive every day.

As do their school-age children, the parents also have their frustrations in the new culture. The father feels that life here is too uncertain and insecure, and the mother is self-conscious of her difference. According to Mr. Savang:

Here the life is better. You can make a lot of money and buy everything. But you don't know when you would lose the job. If I lose the job, I can't do anything. In Laos, we wouldn't starve if I didn't have a job. We had our own houses. I could go fish in Mekong River or go hunting. Here if you don't have a job, you have nothing to eat, and no place to stay. You can't do anything.

Paw talks about her mother:

My mother misses being the same as anybody else at home. There she didn't have to worry what she said or how she behaved, nobody would laugh at her. But here she had to be careful about what she said, she did, and she wore.

From what they have said I can tell that the Savangs' life in their new country is not easy for them. The greatest difficulty, as Mr. Savang said, is, "We don't know the rules and regulations of this country."

Take the insurance for example. The book says that if I don't want to stay with the company, I can just discontinue the payment. But when I stopped the payment, the company called me all the time, saying I would be in big trouble. I don't know why, I did according to what the book said. The same as when I rented the apartment. The landlord said that only my family could live there, but he complained that we had too many people lived there, but I told him those were all my children. He said that he would take me to the court. I just don't know how to handle those things. Every time when I do something, I read the manual very carefully. It is not easy for me, take days for me to read something. I have to check words in the dictionary all the time. Very often I have to take words to ask my friends about them as the dictionary can't help me. But still I got into trouble all the time, I just don't know why.

Yet, no matter how much they miss their past and how much frustration they have had with their new life, the Savangs have hopes for their future. They trust this country. As Mr. Savang said:

Here if you work hard, you can have the same life as anybody else. But in my country, things are not good. Only the Communist families can go ahead, have good jobs and good life. Now, it's difficult for us, as we just started our life here. Maybe later, we'll be better. I believe if we work hard, we will be okay. I believe the education will help my children to have better life here. But I can't afford to send them all to college. Education is never [too] late. I asked them to work and save money for their own education. I want my children to have the same life as those Americans, having big house, big land, and good cars. I want my children to have easy job [white-collar jobs] and live a long life.

Like their father, the younger children have dreams and wishes. Those dreams and wishes give them strength and hope to endure any hardship they face. To reach the future, they put up with the present. In speaking of his dreams, Tran says:

I dream to have a house by the water and mountains. If I have a lot of money some day, I would like to go back to my own country, to build a house by the lake. I want to help my country and my people. I want to work in the army like my great-grandfather. But I don't know what I really can do. There are so many changes in my life. I can't make any plans, but just wait and see. It depends a lot on my English.

Cham says:

I dream to have a big house with a swimming pool at the back yard, to have a convertible car, fancy house and fancy car, that's my dream. After I work for two or three years, when I have money, I want to visit my country. I don't want to live there, just visit.

Sy says:

I dream to have a rich life, just like rich people here, having a lot of money, good cars, houses, everything, big swimming pool in the back yard. I want to be the master of everything. I don't know about my future. If I can learn English good, I want to be an ESL teacher in the refugee camps in Thailand. I want to help the refugee children to learn English. I am too young, I don't really know what I can do in my future.

Unlike the boys, Paw has more realistic plans. She is a down-to-earth person. She has dreams, but she is caught between her own wishes and the traditional role for girls in the family.

I don't care for money, having a big house, or land. I just want to have a good family, a person who can care for me and love me. You can have money, but that doesn't mean you have happiness no matter where you are. I like a man who is a hard worker and deserves what he does. I don't care he is rich or not. I want to go to college, to be a nurse. But I don't know if I can or not, because of my English. My older brother said that he would pay me to go, and my two older sisters would help me too. But I don't know. My mother doesn't want me to leave the house. They want me to stay home to help them. They are too traditional to let me go away.

The children's own stories and words tell us not only their dreams and wishes, their memories and past experiences, their worries and frustrations, but also their values, their personalities, and their sense of self in the new culture. Their stories are seldom heard by others. People know them only as quiet and shy refugee children who speak broken English. They have few chances to express themselves at school. "Some of those kids wouldn't even speak ten words a day at the school," says Jane, their ESL teacher. Once we give them a chance to talk, or give ourselves a chance to listen to them, we would find these children similar to any other youngsters around us: full of ideas and opinions, full of dreams and wishes, and full of the puzzles and uncertainties of the world they live in. Of course, coming to a new culture, Tran, Cham, Paw, and Sy have a far more challenging life than others their age. And of all the things in the new culture that they have to adjust to, the most challenging is their life at school.

Chapter Two

At the Edge of the New Culture

It is as if we walk on stage into a play whose enactment is already in progress—a play whose somewhat open plot determines what parts we may play and toward what denouements we may be heading. Others on stage already have a sense of what the play is about, enough of a sense to make negotiation with a newcomer possible.

—Jerome Bruner, *Acts of Meaning*

Standing far from center stage, Tran, Cham, Paw, and Sy, like any newcomers, are wondering, trying to figure out the contours of their new stage. It is so unfamiliar, so different from their old one. They are trying to define their positions, the parts they might play on this new stage. They cannot, nor do they want to, discard their past, but they need to find a way to survive as the selves they choose to be in the new environment. One thing they all believe is that if they do well at school, they will succeed in their new culture.

One day in February, I took Cham and his twenty-year-old sister, Mei, to swim in the pool at my college. They had swum in the lake at the back of their house in Laos all year round, but they had never used an indoor pool before. Cham jumped into the pool immediately and swam like a crazy fish. But Mei walked to the pool from the locker room with all her clothes on. She had brought her swim suit with her, but she refused to change. She said she just wanted to watch the others swim.

The walls of the room were lined with benches. First Mei sat near the shallow end of the pool, where many children were playing in the water with their parents. Ten minutes later, she moved to the bench in the middle. She did not talk or smile, just sat there quietly and watched. A few minutes later she moved again, to sit on the bench near the deep end where Cham was swimming. She did not talk to him; she just watched. Then she changed her seat again. In twenty minutes, she had circled around the whole pool and had watched the swimmers from the four sides of the room. Then she quietly went back to the locker room and came out a few minutes later wearing a T-shirt over her swim suit. She jumped into the water where many children were and swam there until we left. Both Cham and Mei told me they had a good time.

Mei's behavior before she jumped into the pool typifies how newcomers first enter a new culture. Before she took action, she observed carefully. On the edge of the water, she tried to figure out what the others were doing and where it was safe for her to be. When she was reasonably confident in her new environment, she started to act in it. She chose the safer place to begin. And she acted according to her own sense of what was appropriate to her: by keeping her T-shirt on while she swam. (In Lao culture, women and girls are not sup- posed to expose their bodies in public.)

A school is far more complicated than a swimming pool. Tran, Cham, Paw, and Sy have too many customs to figure out, too many sides from which to view life, and too many adjustments to make. Like Mei, they remain at the edge in order to observe and makes sense of what is going on. But in contrast to Mei, they are given no time to wait before they act. They must act and think how to do it at the same time.

Aside from one or two periods a day in the ESL rooms, Tran, Cham, Paw, and Sy spend most of their time with other American students in classrooms. Most of the classes they attend are on the lowest track, B level (C level: college bound; A level: average; B level: below average). Students who are labelled as either school failure or low motivated learner are marginalized learners. All four demonstrate the following characteristics of being marginalized learners:

- They sit alone, away from others, or with the people with whom they identify.
- They seldom initiate conversation.
- They rarely join any interaction unless they are called upon.
- They appear indifferent to others' conversation and interactions (their faces show no expression, or their heads are turned away from action or lowered).

Because of this kind of behavior, all four siblings appear the same when they are among their American peers. Once I got to know them, however, I could recognize their individual qualities. From my observations and interviews, I can provide the following descriptions:

Tran tends to sit in the corner, near the quietest student in the class. He never speaks up and seldom interacts with others. Sometimes he whispers to his neighbor. But he smiles all the time. When Tran is teased, he smiles back. When he is called on, he smiles before he gives an answer. When he is embarrassed, he smiles with a blush. When he listens to others' chat, he has a smile on his face. But when someone is being teased or laughed at, he never smiles but looks as if he does not know what to do. It would appear that Tran does not belong to the community, as he never joins any conversation or laughs with the crowd. But he says he wishes he could be part of the community, though sometimes he does not like the way his peers talk.

Cham likes his desk to be far away from others at the back of the room. Yet he is alert to everything. His head is always up whenever there is some noise in the room. He listens to others' talk, though it seems he cannot understand it most of the time. But when he understands, he reacts immediately. For instance, Cham will laugh with the others. He does not mind being called on by the teacher, and he gives his answers loudly if he is sure of them. He is bold and tries to join in. The hardest thing for Cham is to take part in conversations because, he says, "I don't understand what they say." But he really wants to belong: "I wish I could just do like them."

Paw seats herself differently in different classes. In science class, she always sits by herself at the end of the table near the door. In English class, she sits with Carol, her only American friend, who does not have any other friends in the school. In math class, she is assigned to sit with her group. Paw never looks around, seldom speaks, rarely even whispers to her neighbor. When there is some activity in the room, she turns her head away from it. She covers half of her face most of the time. When she has to speak, she covers her mouth and her eyes look down. She ignores any noise or activity in the room and concentrates on her own work. Academically, Paw resembles her peers: she'd like to get an A in everything. But socially she chooses to be different, apart from them. She says firmly, "I don't want to be like them. I just want to be myself."

Sy appears to be a loner. In class, he always sits by himself: in the front, at the back, or in the corner. Even when the class sits in a circle on the floor, he will sit a foot away from the others. He lowers his head most of the time, even when listening to others. Once in a while he raises his head, looks around, then immediately lowers it again. He appears shy, timid, and passive. When someone approaches him, he first looks at the person from the corner of his eye, without raising his head. If it is somebody he likes, he smiles and says, "What's up?" or gives a high five. If it is somebody he does not like, he keeps his head down and continues what he is doing, ignoring the person. Sy appears not to care about belonging, but in fact, he says, "I wish I could do everything like them—talk, laugh, and act, just everything, but I don't know how."

All four siblings are on the edge of their new culture, trying to be part of it. Tran associates himself with his peers through his constant polite smile. Cham wants to try whatever his peers do. Paw is determined to resemble the others academically, though she reserves herself socially. Sy has a burning desire to be just like his peers, although he appears to wait passively for opportunities.

How long will they remain at the edge? Will their education help them get acquainted with their new culture and feel part of it? Looking at the details of how each of the four acts in class can lead us closer to the answers to these questions.

Tran

Nineteen-year-old Tran is a gentleman, quiet, polite, and thoughtful. Once he gets to know and like you, he can be very talkative. He likes to express his opinions on just about everything. But in the classroom, you can hardly see or hear him.

12:50 P.M.

Tran walks into the biology class five minutes before the class starts. He sits at the end of a table next to David. Before he sits down, he gives David a smile. This is the B level biology class. There are nine students, seven boys and two girls. Before the class starts, the students are chatting:

> Student 1 (*talking to a student across the room*): I saw you on the street last night. Are you a street roamer?
> Student 2: No, I tried to get some pizza.
> Student 1: But I saw you using the pay phone all the time.

Ann walks into the room. David says something to her. Nobody notices them until Ann suddenly yells out at David, "Good for you, I'm going to kick your butt off." Her sudden roar quiets down the room noise for a few seconds. Ann walks angrily to her seat next to Lila. David lowers his head and blushes. Tran has a shocked and tense expression on his face. The others resume their chat.

Another student walks into the room. Before he puts his bag at the table by the door, he lets out a loud cry: "This table is gross. It has pus on it." He walks to the sink to wet a sponge.

The teacher comes into the room. She stands in the front and waits for the students to settle down. When she sees the student at the sink, she says to him, "John, would you please not use that sink?" He replies, "I'm going to clean the table. There is some pus on it." The teacher turns to the class and says, "We are going to do some pretests." The students respond:

37

Student 1: Oh, no!
Student 2 (*in a dragging, sleepy tone*): Wait, let me get my red pen.
Student 3: Can I go to my locker?

When all the students have settled down, the teacher goes through the items in the pretest one by one. Ken volunteers the most answers. Two or three students yell out their answers once in a while. One student stares absently at nowhere the whole time. Tran and David never raise their hands or their voices, they whisper to each other about their work. Soon the pretest is over.

1:15 P.M.

The teacher gives out some worksheets. She works through them question by question, and the students take turns giving the answers. One set of worksheets is completed this way.

1:30 P.M.

The second set of worksheets is handed to the students. The teacher goes through the same procedure.

1:40 P.M.

The third set of worksheets is distributed. Ken speaks up loudly to the teacher, who is standing at the front of the room.

Ken: Do we have more worksheets to do after this?
Teacher: I'll see how many we'll have to do.
John: Just dash them on.
Student 1: In a few seconds, I will forget them all.
Student 2: I forget what I did yesterday.
Ken: I won't.
Student 1: What did you do yesterday?

Despite the students' interaction, the teacher goes through the third set of worksheets the same way as the first two. Many students start to yawn loudly. There are only five minutes left to the period. The teacher lets the students finish the last part on their own. Ken is talking to himself while doing his work: "Does it show what color they are? Oh, yes, they did. It's red." Another student tries to figure out the points he can get. "I got three here, I might lose one in that one. . . . I might get a B, that's not too bad." John finishes his work and starts to talk: "I lost everything in my computer last night. I hit the wrong button, it blanked, saying du . . . du . . . , then nothing was there any more." Another student joins in. "That happened to me once." The teacher smiles at their chat and volunteers, "You never know what they will do to you, those computers."

Tran is concentrating on his work. Sometimes he turns to his neighbor, David, and asks some questions; afterwards, he turns right back to his work. Sometimes he raises his head and listens for a few seconds to the others chatting; then he lowers his head to his worksheet again. The bell rings. Tran is the last one to put his worksheet into the box on the teacher's desk. The teacher asks him, "How are you doing, Tran?" Tran shakes his head and replies with a smile, "I don't know. I am not sure about some parts." He says "See you" to the teacher and leaves the room.

Tran's Behavior and Thoughts

During the entire period, Tran has talked only about the classwork. He whispers to his neighbor about the work and gives the answers when it is his turn. He appears the most left out when his classmates are freely interacting with each other or with the teacher. It is easy for people to think that it is because of his difficulties with English that Tran does not join the conversation. Actually, there is more to it than just the language, as he says:

> I don't like to interrupt teachers. If I have questions I would ask the teacher after the class. I don't like to take time away from the class. Sometimes I wish I could be just like them [his American peers]. They know everything of this country. They know how to interact with teachers and other students. If I was born here, I could do just the same as other American students. But I can't. In class, I don't know how to say. I was not born here. I don't know what and how I should say.

39

Tran does not belong to the community partly because of his language deficiencies, but mostly because of the behavior of his peers, which conflicts with his own values about school and teachers. He faithfully follows the teacher's instructions. He acts immediately on what he is asked to do in class. But many of his peers start conversations when they are asked to work. He is bothered by such behavior.

> In Lao school, we just work and study, we don't fool around. Here they talk, make fun of you, talk about others behind their back all the time.

According to Tran's home culture, students should not chat during class time. That is not the appropriate time to talk, nor is it the way he believes he should behave:

> In my culture, men don't do small talk. We only talk about big things, important things. Here people talk too much, fool around.

But it does not mean that he does not want to have any relationships with Americans. He is hungry for friendship. He wants to know Americans and American culture:

> It's so difficult to have relationship with Americans. I don't know why, it's just hard. I don't know if they like me or not, or what I should say to them. I wish I could live with an American family to know them, know how they live and how they think. Been here for almost three years, I know nothing, or not much about them at all.

School is virtually the only place for young immigrants such as Tran to be among Americans. Most of his classes are tracked at the lowest level; consequently, he spends all his time among marginal students. He assumes these students are typical Americans and generalizes their behavior as the standard for all American young people.

> Here people tell bad things. I don't want to learn that kind of language from them. I want to learn good English from books. Books don't laugh at me. Here if you don't speak well, they laugh at you. So I don't speak to them. Actually I don't know

what they talk about most of the time. I don't understand them, as I never study those words. I can tell [the meaning] from their gestures and tones. I don't want to learn those bad words. Because if I know them, then they say those words to me, that would bother me. I simply don't know what they talk about. I don't want to learn to say those words.

Sinclair and Ghory (1987) define marginal learners as "people in difficulty who are reacting to unfavorable school conditions. They are young people making self-defeating efforts to form a stable connection between themselves and the educational setting" (p. 181). Such students tend to release their anger and resistance in rebellious ways. Of course, they may be American, but they do not represent all Americans. Unfortunately for Tran, a newcomer who knows so little about American people and American culture, what he sees and hears most of the world he has come to join comes from young people who are alienated themselves. What he learned previously about American society ("America is a rich and democratic country where everybody can do what he or she wants to do and be what he or she wants to be") made him eager for American culture, but his experience of the reality day by day makes him resist being part of it. His lack of knowledge of the new culture and his resistance to being part of it keep him on the margin of the marginalized group with whom he is associated.

Tran believes that education will help him move ahead. "I know education is important to us," he says. "We came to this new country, we need education to help us." His father holds the same belief: "Education can help my children to get good jobs and live like other Americans." With this thought in mind, Tran patiently bends his head to those worksheets that flood his desk. He seldom complains and he wastes no time. He tries hard to do what he was asked to do, to get good grades, and to finish all the assignments on time.

Tran works constantly in class and during other school time. He takes no breaks, not even for lunch. Almost every day during lunchtime, he sneaks into Andy's ESL room to do his schoolwork. Andy leaves school at 11:30 A.M. every day. That is why Tran can hide in Andy's room. According to the school rules, students are not allowed to stay in any rooms during lunchtime. Tran knows the rule, but he simply needs the time.

Lunchtime is normally the best time for students to associate with each other, but Tran feels he cannot afford the time. Most of the time he shuts himself in the ESL room to finish assignments. But do his efforts help him join his new culture, fulfill his dream, or ultimately become what he wants to be in this new world? When he first came to the United States, he thought so, but now he doubts it. Although he has studied in the American school for almost three years, he still does not speak, read, and write English well, no matter how hard he tries. He has begun to doubt his intelligence:

> In Laos, we memorized everything. I could remember very well. I just could remember everything. But here I know I am dumb. My trouble is my English. I just couldn't learn it well. I don't know why.

Tran is constantly exposed to English, but he has little opportunity to speak it. At school he is either too confused or too busy to speak. He spends all his time working silently and alone on those motionless and soundless worksheets. He previously thought, "If I work hard, I can do well," but after working this way for almost three years, Tran is disappointed in the amount of progress he has made. Jerome Bruner (1986) posits:

> Language is acquired not in the role of spectator but through use. Being "exposed" to a flow of language is not nearly so important as using it in the midst of "doing." Learning a language, to borrow John Austin's celebrated phrase, is learning "how to do things with words." The child is not learning simply what to say but how, where, to whom, and under what circumstances. (p. 75)

Seeing how Tran learns English at school, I realized he studied English for grades and tests, but rarely used it for real communicative purpose. He has begun to lose his trust in the type of education he is receiving:

> Here what I learn in the school will only help me a little bit for my future. What I learn in the school is only to help me learn how to contact people here, not a lot, only a little bit. Everything I learn now I will forget soon.

He started on the margin and still remains on the margin, both socially and academically, after three years of hard work in the school. He has become impatient and frustrated with himself. He blames himself for his marginality. His ESL teacher, Jane, worries about him:

> He has a low self-image. He told me that he was a very successful student back in Laos, a student leader there. But here he can't do anything well. His English is very poor. I have a hard time understanding him. He is frustrated and seems impatient with himself. He wants to see good results immediately. Since he can't do it, he is very frustrated. Sometimes he comes here and doesn't concentrate on what I ask him to do, but likes to talk. He talks fast, writes fast, and it's hard to understand him and his writing. I think that is his way to cover his problems, by talking a lot and shuffling pages all the time. He just can't settle down to study.

When Tran first came to the United States, he thought confidently, "If I had English, I could do anything." But after three years of hard work in school, he has lost his confidence:

> I want everything in life to be in control. But now everything is fifty percent uncertain, actually nothing is certain. I don't know what I can do or what I want to be. It all depends on my English. If my English is good, I can make plans, but now I don't know.

Tran is still trying hard. In isolation, he silently bends his head to the many worksheets he faces daily. He assumes that the cause of his marginality lies within himself. He expresses no complaints, but works hard.

Paw

Like Tran, sixteen-year-old Paw studies silently and hard in isolation all the time, but she is more persistent and patient with her work than Tran, because she has very clear goals for her learning: "I want to go to college, to be a nurse." The following description of Paw's English class shows where Paw locates herself in the class, and how she behaves among her peers, communicates with the teacher, and acts as a student generally.

9:15 A.M.

Paw walks into the English class and sits next to Carol in the front row. This is a B level English class. The class has eight students, five boys and three girls. Three of the students are Laotian.

Paw sits with one hand supporting her head; her eyes look blank as she waits for the class to start. She looks tired. By her side, Carol is busy writing words from the vocabulary sheet. The other students are chatting with each other. Once in a while Paw briefly turns her eyes to the students who are chatting happily, then immediately comes back to herself. When those students laugh loudly, Paw turns her head toward the crowd and gives a faint smile, which is hardly detectable, as her mouth is mostly covered by her left hand.

9:20 A.M.

The teacher speaks to the class in a firm voice: "I will give you half an hour to check your spelling words and vocabulary. This is study time, so no conversation." Paw has her eyes fixed on the desk; she listens while the teacher is talking. As soon as the teacher ends the instructions, Paw takes out the vocabulary sheet from a folder and starts to work on it.

Tim, a boy sitting by the window, slams his bag on the desk hard. That makes a very loud noise. The teacher turns her head and looks at him, but says nothing. John has his face in his arms and does not move until the teacher calls for his attention. Brian yells out, "You push too hard!" while staring at the teacher. The teacher ignores him.

Carol and Mimi help each other memorize the words on the vocabulary sheet. Paw works by herself.

9:35 A.M.

The teacher stands in the front of the room waiting for the students to get ready for the quiz. Carol and Mimi are still working on their vocabulary. Paw puts the spelling and vocabulary sheets back into the folder and, with a pencil in her hand, waits for the test to begin.

The first part of the test is dictation. The teacher reads a paragraph from a health magazine, sentence by sentence, to the class. She stops when she sees John put his pen down and shake his head. "Where are you, John?" she asks. "Read that sentence with *confinement* again, please?" he asks. The teacher repeats the sentence. She then goes on. Tim groans aloud with frustration. The teacher stops for him. She repeats the sentence and goes on. Another boy gives a heavy sigh and asks the teacher, "What's the word before *substitute*?" "*Prevailing*," the teacher answers him. The dictation lasts twenty-five minutes.

Before the second part of the test, the teacher goes around the class to check how the students are doing with their dictation. Paw raises her hand. When the teacher comes to her, Paw says, almost in a whisper and with her eyes fixed on her paper, "I didn't hear the word before the word *dog*." "Oh, that's *prairie*," the teacher tells her. "Thank you," Paw whispers back.

After the teacher finishes checking everyone's dictation, she gives out the second part of the quiz. It is a multiple-choice vocabulary test.

While everybody is quietly taking the test, the teacher sits at her desk correcting the work the students have just done. Suddenly the teacher calls out Paw's name. "Paw, you owe me some work?" Paw raises her head and answers the teacher in a very soft voice. "Yes, I was sick," she says, then immediately lowers her head again. Paw gives a deep sigh, which could only be heard by someone sitting close to her.

The class is over. One by one, the students walk to the front and leave their work on the teacher's desk. John drags his feet out of the room, his body swinging from side to side. Ryan lets his worksheet fly onto the teacher's desk without even looking at how it lands. Paw remains at her desk, working.

After everybody is gone, Paw stands up and goes to the front of the room. In a low voice, with her eyes looking down, she says, "I'm not done." The teacher looks up at her and says firmly, "You finish it here, then go to the ESL room." Paw goes back to her seat. She has only half of the work done. With her pen, she points to each word on the sheet, murmuring to herself. She stops at one word for a few seconds, then moves to the next and comes back to the previous word again. The teacher notices her and says, "Paw, do those you know." Paw has already done those she knows; the ones left are those she is not sure of. Paw does not say anything or raise her head but continues her murmuring, going from unknown to unknown.

Finally, she moves to the last section. She struggles with *confinement* and *confine*. She does not know the difference between them and cannot decide the places for each of them. She writes *confine* first in one blank, and *confinement* in another. Then, thinking that might be wrong, she erases the two words and changes their places. She does not feel that is right either, and she erases them again. Over and over she tries one way and then another. Finally, she just puts them down at random. In that empty room, alone at her seat, Paw struggles silently, with the teacher soundlessly sitting at the front desk correcting the students' work and giving them grades.

It is time for Paw to leave the room. She fills the empty blanks in a hurry and puts the sheet on the teacher's desk. With a deep sigh, she returns to her seat and packs her things into her bag. She walks out of the room silently, with her head bent and her eyes looking downward.

Soundlessly she walks through the crowd in the hallway with her head bent slightly, not looking at anyone. Quietly and unresponsively, she passes by students who are laughing, yelling, bumping into each other, talking, and shouting in the hall.

Paw's Behavior and Thoughts

During the fifty minutes of the English class, all Paw spoke were three sentences: one question asking a word in the dictation, one in response to the teacher's request, and one to tell the teacher that she had not finished her work. The three sentences were all short, and she said them in a voice so soft it was as if the words had a hard time getting out of her. Paw did not speak to any of her classmates, not even to Carol sitting next to her, the person Paw considers her only friend in the school. It seems that she is afraid to be heard and noticed. When she is not working, one of her hands always covers half of her face, as though she is trying to hide behind it. Not only does she not intend to join any conversation in the room, but she turns her head away from the noise, indicating that she wants no part of it. She does not like to make any noise in public. In her home culture, as a girl, she is not supposed to talk.

> In my culture, girls are not supposed to talk too much, or make any noise. Otherwise, they don't think you are nice. When I was little, I liked to talk a lot. Once my father yelled at me: "Nobody likes to hear you, and nobody wants to listen to you!" Since then, I never like to talk.

Not only does she not like to be heard in public, but she is also bothered very much by how her peers behave in the class. She complains:

> The least I like about the school is the kids here. Because they don't respect their friends, don't respect their teachers, and newcomers. They tease them, make fun of them, and fool around.
>
> In Laos, you are not allowed to talk back to the teacher, have to do what they say. If you don't get things done, they would hit you.

Paw was brought up very differently from her American peers. As a girl, she was not supposed to be noticed in public. She is passive and not used to arguing with anybody, especially the authorities:

> It's easy for me when the teacher asks me to answer questions instead of me raising hands. When the students have a big argument, especially talk back to the teacher, I don't know what I should do. I am not used to that. I can only be quiet.

Politeness and respect for others are highly valued by her home culture. In the lower-level high school classes, she sees an extreme side of her new culture. But, like Tran, she generalizes this extreme as "the American kids":

> They are yelling, calling names, talking about their boy- or girlfriends all the time. I am not used to students interrupting teachers in the class, not used to arguing with the teacher, or talking about other things when they should work.

Paw is determined not to become like them. She is also annoyed by some other Laotian students who imitate their American peers:

> I don't want to be like them at all. I seldom speak to them unless I have to. I saw some Lao students who have some American friends. They have to talk and do as their friends do when they are together with them. I don't like that. That's not my way. If that's the case to have friends, I prefer to have none

Paw does not mean that she resents all American young people. She says that she wants to have American friends, but she wants "only to make friends with the people who understand you, care about your feelings, and are polite." She has one American friend, Carol, whom she likes very much. Like Paw, Carol is a loner at school. Paw sympathizes with her: "She [Carol] was nice, but the others don't like her and pick on her all the time. I don't know why."

Socially, Paw chooses to be on the fringe and refuses to be assimilated, because what she sees of the new culture goes against her values. But academically, she wants to be like her peers. The fact that she is behind most of them in class bothers her tremendously. Unlike Tran, she does not diagnose herself as being "dumb," but she persistently tries and never gives up. When she has problems with the English assignment, the teacher asks her to do only part of it. She refuses the offer. She does not only the entire assignment but also the extra, bonus section.

When she had a hard time finishing the U.S. history homework, the teacher suggested that she do only two-thirds of it, yet promised to give her full credit. But Paw said no. "Then," she says, "how can I take the same test with them [her class], if I don't do the same exercises with them?"

Paw works very hard. Besides cooking dinner for the family every day, she spends all her time doing schoolwork. Very often she works until midnight. She has no free weekend or holiday time and no time for any physical exercise, so she often gets sick. Her absences from illness drag her further behind. Then she has to work still harder. But schoolwork does not bother her as much as housework. She says, "I wish I didn't have so much housework, then I could spend more time on my schoolwork."

For three years, Paw has tried very hard in all the subjects she has studied in school. She says, "I don't have too many exciting things in my life. The most exciting thing for me is to get good grades. I want all A's for everything." Every time she takes a test in English, she is the last one to leave the room. Every day she memorizes the words in the vocabulary book, few of which she has ever heard. She believes that memorizing those words will help her speak English better.

Paw is struggling on the edge, but she is determined to succeed in school. After three years of studying in America, she has made tremendous progress as a literate person. When she first came here she was almost illiterate, both in Lao and in English. Now, through hard work, she manages to keep up with eleventh-grade work. Aside from English, where she remains at the lowest level, she is either in the high or the middle ranks in her other subjects.

For Paw, the worst part of English lies in speaking it, because that is what she does the least every day. Like Tran, she has little time and few chances to speak English, either in school or at home. Talk, as Britton (1972) believes, is the most likely means by which students first investigate, explore, and organize new fields of interest. Unfortunately, Paw spends all her time with her head lowered, working on soundless vocabulary sheets, and still the words remain strange to her. Quite often, she is humiliated with the spelling tests and leaves the classroom dismayed. As a poor English speaker, she continues to struggle on the margin. Though she will not change her mind about going to college, she expresses her worries:

> I don't know whether I can get into college because of my English. I'll have to take TOEFL [Test of English as a Foreign Language], and I am worried about that test. I am not sure I can do it well in order to get into the college.

The implication of what Paw says is that she does not think she has improved her English as much as she wants. She is most concerned about tests. She connects academic achievement with doing well on tests. That is the message she receives in school. Frank Smith (1986) has criticized the common practice of teaching and learning for tests in American schools. He states that students are the direct victims of this practice: "Often the results of tests can move students out of the 'mainstream'—the term is educational jargon again—into side channels from which they can rarely escape" (p. 143). Students study for tests and are classified by the scores they attain on those tests. By being put at the bottom level in her English class, Paw is conscious of her low status at school. She is worried. She does not know why she works so hard, yet still cannot use the language well enough to achieve her goal: passing tests and going to college.

Cham

In many ways, seventeen-year-old Cham appears the same as Tran and Paw in the classroom: quiet, businesslike, and alone.

But he is very different from them in terms of his personality. He is not shy among strangers, he is very active, and he tries to seize every chance to have fun. In the following description, Cham shows himself to be quite interested in what goes on around him although, like Tran and Paw, he is still separated from the crowd.

11:06 A.M.

The scene is science class, B level, general science. There are twelve students, five girls and seven boys. Cham walks into the room and seats himself at a table near the door by himself. Other students are in pairs or groups, chatting. The teacher chats with the students. Cham takes something out of his folder and starts to read it. But he is watching and listening to the others at the same time.

> Student 1: I went to the dance last night.
> Student 2: Did you? Who did you go with?
> Student 3: With a guy?
> Student 2: Did you go there to find a guy?
> Student 4: Probably not only one guy, but two or three.
> Student 1: Yeah, then I can have [a] choice to make.

Everybody in the group laughs. Cham hears them and laughs hard too, though he does not seem to understand much of the others' interaction. Very often when the others laugh, he has a puzzled expression on his face, but he immediately joins their laughter when he understands them.

11:10 A.M.

The class starts. The teacher walks to Cham and asks him, "Have you made copies of your piece?" Cham shakes his head. The teacher's aide, who is sitting next to a boy in a wheelchair, walks over, takes Cham's science report from his hand, and walks out of the room. Soon she is back with photocopies. She gives one copy to Cham and the rest to the teacher.

It is current events time. Everyone takes turns sharing the current event he or she has read from a newspaper or magazine. One boy talks about the war in Iraq. Another shares his reading about AIDS research. "I heard that white people are more susceptible to AIDS," one student says. A girl says, "Be careful, that is racist." More discussion on the issue follows.

Cham reads his own piece silently while the others talk. He is listening too, but it is hard to tell whether he understands anything, as his expression remains impassive. Then comes Cham's turn. The teacher distributes to the class the copies of Cham's piece that the teacher's aide just made.

Cham reads his current event. The class is very quiet as he reads. The current event he shares is about a dentist's invention of certain tubes that will prevent dolphins and whales from coming close to the beaches. Cham reads each word slowly and carefully. After his reading, the teacher immediately compliments him: "Good, Cham. I've just learned about this. I didn't know dolphins would come to the beach too. I thought only whales would do that. That's very good. Thank you." No response from the students. They are very quiet. When the teacher compliments him, Cham lowers his head, blushes, and says nothing.

11:30 A.M.

Today the teacher talks about the earth, the weather changes on the earth, the distance and the angle of the earth from the sun. He asks three boys to come to the front of the room, to be the sun, the earth, and the moon, and he moves the boys around as he explains the distance and the angle between them. The three boys make faces to the class, and one boy exaggerates his movement by falling down flat on the one next to him. The class laughs, and Cham laughs hard too.

11:50 A.M.

Ten minutes before the class is over, the teacher gives an assignment: to find an article on science and write about it. He points to a table by the wall. "I have some articles there," he says. "Go there to see whether there are some you are interested in." Many students stand up and go to the table.

Cham leaves his seat and goes to the table too. The table is crowded. Cham stands a foot away, waiting. When two students leave the table, he steps closer to it and flips from one article to another from the stack on the table. Two minutes later, he finds one and takes it back to his seat. He starts to read it. Cham quietly reads by himself at his desk near the door, while the others talk loudly in groups or from across the desks; some move around from desk to desk.

The class is over. The students chat and laugh on their way out of the room. Cham packs his things into his bag and goes to the teacher, who is talking to a student. Next to the teacher, Cham listens to the conversation between the teacher and the student, his body slightly bent over. When the teacher finishes talking, he turns to Cham and says, "Cham, nice job for the current event." Cham does not say anything; he does not smile. He gives a paper he did last night to the teacher and says, "This is the paper. Can I get it back today?" The teacher takes it, looks at the half page filled with words, and says, "Is this it?" Cham replies, "Yeah." "Okay," says the teacher. "Come to me after school." Cham nods his head and leaves the room.

Cham's Behavior and Thoughts

Like Tran and Paw, Cham is quiet in the classroom. He seldom speaks up or interacts with anyone. Physically he sets himself apart from the community. Tran and Paw choose to sit next to the students they identify with, but Cham always sits by himself, away from anyone else. But he listens to the others' conversation and watches what is happening around him. He expresses his reactions openly and seldom tries to hide his feelings.

He is less shy among the crowd and less concerned about what others think of him than Tran and Paw. For instance, Tran and Paw never voluntarily read anything to the class. They are too afraid that no one will understand them and they will appear "dumb" to the others. But Cham is different. In the beginning, the teacher would read the current event Cham prepared because of Cham's strong accent. After a few weeks, Cham told the teacher that he wanted to try to read his report by himself. In order for the class to understand him, he made copies of what he would read for the class. The first time he read his current event to the class, he was very excited. He later told the ESL teacher, Jane, that he was nervous but he "felt good about himself," though he did not know how much his class understood him.

The teacher is the only person in the class who talks to Cham; no one else does. Like Tran and Paw, Cham appears left out when the students interact freely with each other. During these times, he takes out some reading or work to do while the others talk. But his head is often upright as he listens and watches his peers. He joins their laughter when he understands them. But he seldom initiates contact with them. After a few months of being in the class, I asked him whether he knew any of the names of his classmates. He shook his head and said, "Maybe one or two, those the teachers called the most. Only their first names, and I am not sure of their last names."

Cham is not a talker. He associates himself with others by doing things with them, rather than sharing thoughts or ideas with them. Unlike Tran, he seldom complains that he has no friends or is looked down upon by the others in school. He has become friends with a Mexican student in the ESL room, and they often do things together after school. He is very happy for that. Very often he takes Sy to Woodland Drive to play sports with their Laotian friends. Cham enjoys his American school much more than he enjoyed his Laotian school. He thinks the former is much more fun than the latter. He states:

> I often skipped school in Laos. It was so boring: read, memorize, read, memorize, that was all you do every day. The teachers were not nice. They hit us, yelled at us, and punished us hard. I like American schools much better. You can do things here. I like to make things with my hands. Here we have big gym, computer, and everything. The teachers are nicer. Time passes faster in the school than at home.

The most difficult thing for Cham is interacting with American students. He says he does not know how to interact with them, and he is not used to talking to the teacher on an equal level. But he enjoys listening to the students and is interested in how they interact with each other. He hopes some day to "just do like them when my English is good." But he sets limits for his personal behavior. He says, "The students should obey the teachers. They shouldn't argue with the teacher, shouldn't interrupt the teacher in the class, that is not good."

Cham seems more open to his new culture than Tran and Paw, though he is still bound by his old cultural values in many ways. He says he could never kiss or hug a girl in public, but he would not mind watching others do it. He even drew a picture of a boy and a girl kissing and hugging each other for a Valentine's Day assignment in art class. Knowing Tran and Paw, I can imagine that they would be very embarrassed and turn away if they accidentally caught some boys or girls kissing or hugging.

Cham is good in sports and in doing things with his hands. He won first prize—five hundred dollars—for a Musical Chairs game in town, and he also won first prize for the rocket he made as an assignment in science class. From TV, he learns how Americans enjoy skiing, skating, bowling, swimming, taking trips, and playing Nintendo. He wants to try them all. He is interested in the TV game show *Wheel of Fortune* and has asked how one becomes a contestant on the show. He wants to win a car. He talks about applying for a credit card and renting a car to travel all over the country.

In the Savang family, Cham is unique. His brothers and sister have different opinions about him. Tran sneers at him, saying, "He wanted to be somebody that he even didn't know of." Paw sees him as "too self-concerned. Only cares about himself but not others." But Sy enjoys him: "Cham is the only one among my brothers and sisters who will play games with me or take me out to have fun."

In Cham's opinion, the best parts of American culture are taking trips on the weekends, playing games, boating, and going to parties. He dreams of not having to work, having lots of money and a beautiful house, going to parties, and having a good time every day. He is influenced by TV, the conversations among his American peers, and his favorite reading material: *People* magazine. When I asked him what his opinion of the American people was, he answered:

> There is a good part and also a bad part of them. The good part is they help people; the bad part is they were killing, robbing people. I see that on TV every day.

Among the three high school students in the family, Cham has the most difficulty with his studies. He is in the lowest level in every subject. He takes math individually with the teacher, since he can hardly understand anything in the class. Before he moved down to a lower-level English class in the tenth grade, he was reading and doing different assignments from the rest of his class. In science class, he often simply writes down the things that the teacher writes on the board, because he cannot understand much of what the teacher and other students say.

Cham depends very much on the ESL tutors to help him to get through his reading and writing assignments. But he is patient with himself and seldom gets frustrated or depressed over being behind. His favorite subjects are science and art because he enjoys doing things with his hands. He knows English is important, but he does not know how to improve his English. He does whatever he is asked and gets every assignment done on time. Still, he is behind everyone in the class. When I asked him whether he thought that his studies today would prepare him for his future life in this country, he replied:

> Maybe, they said that if you know more, then they pay you more. I don't know what subjects will help me for my future. Maybe English; if I can speak well, and know more English, I can get a good job. I like to study the things that can help me get jobs. I know I want to do some mechanic or electronic jobs. I heard that they pay well. That is why I want to go to the vocational school to study those things.

Unlike Tran and Paw, Cham does not have a very clear idea of what courses he needs to take. Tran likes math, and Paw prefers English, but Cham will "take anything that would help me get good jobs." He thinks that once he has a job and makes a lot of money, he will be able to live like other Americans and do whatever he wants to do. Today he works very hard to get through school in the belief that, "with an American high school diploma, I would get a good job." His biggest wish is "to make good money and live like an American, at least eighty percent American."

From what Cham says about American culture, I believe he means mainly the culture he has learned from TV commercials, soap operas, and popular magazines like *People*. He understands that to be American culture, but he has overlooked the underlying democratic values of the society—freedom, equality, and individuality, the fundamental principles this nation is based on and the values for which Cham and his family risked their lives and sacrificed everything. Unfortunately, Cham's schooling in America provides little opportunity for him to learn and experience these cultural values. Many cultural theorists (Spindler and Spindler 1987; Trueba 1988a; Tharp and Gallimore 1989) believe that school activity settings should become instrumental to the attainment of cultural goals, as well as to the expression of cultural values. "School activity settings internalized by teachers as settings help them [students] attain their goals of power, recognition, status and so forth" (Spindler and Spindler 1987, p. 167). But tracked at the B level, Cham spends his time on meaningless vocabulary and reading tests, and has no time to discuss or learn about American culture with his peers. Cham's American schooling also affords little opportunity for him to value his home culture and fails to empower him by helping him understand himself and the world he came to join.

Cham's major purpose in staying in school is to "get a high school diploma." One thing he knows that he must learn well is English; as he says, "I want to learn conversational English, that's to learn to talk. To learn vocabulary and spell words."

He puts a lot of effort into his weekly vocabulary test, but he forgets most of the words very soon after, and seldom uses them in speaking or writing. Cham studies very hard with the dream of becoming a "real American," "at least eighty percent American," but his concept of being an American does not include fundamental American values. Unfortunately, Cham's education in America does little to connect the words he learns at school with the world he wants to be part of.

Sy

Sy, at fourteen the youngest in the Savang family, is in many ways like his brothers and sister, but appears more passive than they. The following classroom description illustrates a sharp contrast between his behavior and his peers'.

9:50 A.M.

Sy walks into English class and takes a seat at the end of the table near a window. The teacher asks the class to write a book review about the books they are reading; while they are writing, she will give each student his or her midterm grade. The teacher stands in front of a long table covered with piles of paper, students' notebooks, and books. She is surrounded by a dozen students who are anxious to find out their grades. She explains to one student what grade he got and why he got it. He listens to the teacher carefully, with his eyes fixed on the piece of paper the teacher holds in her hand. Several pairs of eyes peer over the teacher's shoulders, trying to see what is on the paper, and many heads are clustered around the teacher, trying to hear what she says. The students who cannot get closer to see or hear group themselves a foot or so away from the teacher, chatting, laughing, and teasing each other while waiting for their turn. It takes several minutes for the teacher to go through each person's midterm grade. The following is a typical exchange:

> Student: How come I only get eighty-three points for that?
> Teacher: You didn't turn in the homework once.

Student: When was that?

Teacher: Let me check my notes. Okay, that's on January 19. The homework was discussing the character in your reading.

Student: Oh, I was sick. How many points did you take out for that?

Teacher: Ten points.

Student: Then what happened to the seven points I missed?

Teacher: That's taking out from the work you didn't do that well. (*Pause; student says nothing.*)

Teacher: Any questions?

Student: I'll have to think about it.

Teacher: Okay, you can come back to me. Next, please.

10:10 A.M.

The teacher overhears the talk of a group of students near her. She turns around and snaps, "I don't like to hear you talking about other teachers around me. How do you feel if somebody talks about your friends and colleagues just in front of you? That's not nice."

Her rebuke immediately quiets down those students, as well as the whole class. They all stop what they are doing and look toward the front of the room. Sy looks up for only a second and then returns to his work. The teacher turns back to talk to the student to whom she is giving a grade. The students who have been scolded resume talking, but this time they speak in soft voices that can hardly be heard.

Sy is sitting at his desk all this time writing his book review. He turns the book page back and forth and jots down some notes from the book. He writes a few sentences on one piece of paper, then puts it aside and starts to write on a new piece of paper. Soon his desk is covered with pieces of hardly used paper. Several times he goes to the shelf to get more paper to start over again.

From time to time he looks up to the front where the teacher is. There is still a big crowd surrounding the teacher. Some students are playing games on the computers, while other students stand behind, watching them. Other students are chatting with each other about the grades they just received.

Ryan: What did you get?

Dick: Fifty-five.

Ryan: I have one point higher than you.

Dick: I don't think she is right. A couple of things she didn't figure out right. I should have got more than fifty-five.

Ryan: I missed some classes and didn't turn in my journals.

Dick: I had a vacation too. I know what I didn't do for my report on (*he lifts the big dictionary from the table and puts it down hard*) the Web-ster's In-ter-na-tion-al Dic-tion-a-ry (*stressing each syllable*).

10:20 A.M.

When there are not many students around the teacher, Sy stands up and goes to the front of the room. He stands to the right of the teacher with his head lowered, waiting for his turn. When the teacher finishes talking with one student, she turns to Sy.

Teacher: Okay, Sy, this is what you got. You didn't turn in some of the homework, so I have to give you some zeroes.

Sy: How many zeroes I have?

Teacher: Here, one, two, three.

Sy: Okay, thank you.

Sy leaves the teacher immediately for his seat and starts his work again. Dick walks to Sy and asks him, "What did you get, Sy?" "Sixty-seven," Sy replies. "Wow, that's much higher than me. I bet you feel pretty good about that," Dick says to him. Sy does not say anything or even show any reaction on his face but continues his writing. Dick turns to another boy who has finished talking with the teacher.

Ten minutes before the class is over, the teacher still has a few students around her. Most of the students are moving around; a few are sitting at their seats, talking to each other. Sy puts his pen down and walks up to the teacher again. When the teacher turns to him, he shows her what he has done for his book review.

Teacher: See this word, it should be *d-i-v-e*.

Sy: *D-i-v-e.*

Teacher: Right. Did he survive?

Sy: Yes.
Teacher: Write something about his surviving.
(*Sy nods his head as the teacher reads the rest of his writing.*)
Teacher: That's good. (*She hands Sy's work back to him.*)

Sy takes his writing and goes back to his seat to resume working on it. Two minutes before the class is over, he finishes his book review. He puts it in his folder, takes out his math report, and walks over to Dick, who is on the computer. "Can you type this for me?" he asks Dick. "Twenty-five cents a piece, how is that?" Dick says to Sy before he reads the report. After he sees what it is, Dick yells out, "Math report! No, I am not going to type this for you." Without saying anything, Sy takes his math report back from Dick and returns to his seat.

The bell rings. Sy leaves his seat immediately and practically jumps on one of the computer chairs, which was just vacated a second before. The next period is Sy's study hall time. He uses the whole time typing his math report on the computer.

Sy's Behavior and Thoughts

Sy appears to be a loner. He sits alone in the corner and works by himself all the time, despite all the movement and noise around him. He does talk to the teacher and a peer (Dick), but compared to his peers, Sy is so businesslike: no kidding, no joking, no arguing or gossiping. Almost every student questions the teacher about the points he or she receives for the midterm grade. The teacher expects this. That is why she chooses to talk to each student about his or her work individually. Unlike many of his peers, Sy does not argue with the teacher or complain about what he is given; he simply accepts what he gets. When Dick tries to initiate a conversation with him about their grades, Sy does not show any interest. Sy believes that teachers are authorities, and students "should only obey" and not argue with or complain to them.

Sy got three zeroes for not doing his homework three times. He knows he is at fault so he accepts what he gets, but he does not explain to anybody why he did not do his homework. Every time when the teacher asks him about it, he says, "I forgot," with his head lowered. When I ask him why he sometimes does not do his homework, he tells me that sometimes he is not clear about the assignment, sometimes he cannot do the work by himself, and sometimes he is too busy to get all the work done.

Sy does not like to talk. Being the youngest one in the house, he is only talked to, and he can be ordered around by anyone in the house. In his words, "They [the family members] never chat with me, but just ask me to do this or that. I am too young. They don't think I know anything." He is not used to voicing his own opinions. When I ask him questions, he usually replies, "I don't know." He appreciates the equal relationship between teacher and students in school, and he likes the free and loose behavior of his peers. But he does not know how to behave like them. He says, "I really like their free interactions. I wish I could be just like them, but I can't, and I don't know how." Actually he has tried behaving like one of them, his math teacher tells me:

> At the beginning of last September, Sy was hanging around with Dick. He didn't behave well at all. He joked, talked, and made fun all the time, acting silly and fooling around. Just like Dick. When I asked him to sit still, he acted in a silly way, and aroused the laughter of the class. He wanted to have [the] attention of the class. I was very upset and had a serious talk with him, and also separated him from Dick. Since then he was better and better. He became a serious student.

Seeing how serious, timid, and quiet Sy appears now in the classroom, I can hardly believe that Sy behaved the way the math teacher describes. I ask Sy about this. With his head lowered and his eyes cast down, he tells me:

> I liked Dick before, as he was the only one that came to talk to me. He was funny. I sort of wanted to be like him. But I don't know how. I was silly. Now I won't do it any more. I don't like Dick any more. He picked on me and kicked my butt all the

time. I don't like him, he acts silly, not respect others. He had problems almost with all the subjects, but he is smart, he knows almost everything about computer. Now I don't have any friends.

Sy's words parallel what Bruner (1986) says about construction of self-concept: "People's self-esteem and their self-concept changed in sheer reaction to the kinds of people they found themselves among, and changed even more in response to the positive and negative remarks that people made to them" (p. 109). This is the first year Sy is put in the class with the students who are his age. In the previous two years of schooling in America, he was with students much younger than he, because of his low English ability. He began in the second grade. Then he was moved to the sixth grade for a couple of months and then switched to the fourth grade. Last year, before he transferred to Riverside, he was in the third grade. When he arrived in Riverside, he was placed in the sixth grade. Now he is in the seventh grade and is happy to be with children closer to his age. He wants to be like his peers. He tried to imitate his friend Dick, but his behavior was not approved by the teacher. As a result, Sy withdrew. Since the teacher's rebuke he has been careful about each step he takes. Like a turtle, Sy poked his head out of his shell, but was shocked back into it again. Now he does not know what he should do.

> I want to have American friends, but I don't know how. I can't talk like them because of my English. They talk about others behind their back all the time, I can't do that. They fool around, I don't want to be like them. They hang out all the time, I can't do that. I only go out with my brothers.

Sy, like his siblings, lives between two cultures. It is hard for him to adopt behavior that runs counter to the values by which he was raised. However, Sy does not resent his peers' behavior as consciously as Tran and Paw do. When I ask him whether he is bothered by it, he usually responds with, "No, I am used to them" or "I wish I could do just like them" or "That's okay for them, they are Americans."

Sy's behavior among his peers reminds me of Mei's behavior before she jumped into the swimming pool. No matter what situation he finds himself in, Sy starts by being quiet and by standing a few feet away from the crowd with his head lowered. Slowly, as he finds that he can do as the others do, he will loosen up a little bit. He will smile, or laugh, or give high fives to the people who talk to him. Occasionally, when what he does wins approval and praise, he becomes quite animated. But in the face of disapproval, he will withdraw and become quiet, just as he was at first. Sy's behavior demonstrates how a newcomer enters a new world: he "walk[s] on stage into a play whose enactment is already in progress." As a newcomer, Sy has to figure out what role he should play and what position he should be in before he participates.

Sy is mostly passive among his peers and in the classroom. He seldom initiates conversation, except to ask or answer questions about schoolwork. He tries to avoid conflict; instead, he waits for the right moment to interact. When he wants to talk to the teacher, he waits until the teacher is not needed by the others. When he wants to use the computer, he waits until one is available. He rarely speaks in school. He seldom relies on language to negotiate with anyone for things he wants to do. Instead, he passively waits for an opening.

He works almost every minute in school. Alone, by himself, he tries very hard. In the whole period of English class, he worked on his book report. This is what he wrote:

> The *Hatchet* stories the best book I has been reading, it was about the boy survive in the middle of the forest.
> Brian personalities is was very smart and confusion. he smart when he dive in the water and find something in the plane. confusion when he don't know where he were.
> He very tough boy, when the moose try to kill but the moose can't. Then he [words unclear] destroy Brian shelter but he never give up.

For this short book review, seventy-seven words long, Sy has worked the whole class period, with no talking, in total concentration. The other students worked on the assignment while talking and chatting with their friends. It is not possible for Sy to be like his peers. Sy tries to get his work done at school because he knows that is the only place he can get help from the teacher and have it checked by her to make sure it is right.

To utilize every moment, Sy works in the cafeteria while the others wait for their lunch, and while they wait to be dismissed. He works before class starts while the others are talking or playing. His peers have different opinions about his businesslike manner in school. Some say, "He doesn't like us. He just wants to be by himself." Others say, "I wish I could be just like him. He is so disciplined, and can control himself so well. I wish I could do like him." Some assume that "he must never be able to do his homework at home." His teacher comments, "He is a very focused person. He will get his work done in the amount of time that other students are not able to." It is not easy for Sy to concentrate for such a long time all day long. By the end of the day, he feels extremely tired. When he gets home after school, the first thing he does is take a nap.

After three years of hard study in an American school, Sy has made great strides as a literate person, although he is still far behind his peers in speaking, reading, and writing in English. However, he does not know what his schooling is for. He does not know what his studies will bring him to. At the end of the school year, he is not even sure which grade he will go to the next year, because in the past two years, he has been shifted back and forth between the second grade to sixth grade.

When I ask Sy what he wants to do after he graduates from school, he shakes his head and says, "I don't know. I am too young to think that far. Nobody never asked me, or talked about it in my family. For sure I won't go to college as I can't study." When I ask him what he thinks he is studying for, it takes him a while to understand my question, then he replies, "I don't know. I never think of that. Maybe for English, for me to learn to speak English."

Sy impresses me as a person who seldom has a chance to make any decisions in his life. He lives his life tentatively and waits passively to be led somewhere, but he does not know where. Since birth, his life has been so uncertain that he was never sure what would happen the next day. He is the same way in his studies. He is surrounded by the unknown and does not know what he should do next. His first response to any question is "I don't know" before he starts to think about an actual response. Unlike his brothers and sister, Sy has many years to go before he graduates from high school. I wonder if he will become a more confident person as he continues through future years of learning in the school in his new culture.

Tran, Paw, Cham, and Sy stand at the edge of the new culture, observing, learning, and working at becoming part of it. In the eyes of others, they are alike: the Laotians, the refugees, the students who cannot speak much English. They are silent, obedient, hard workers. Because of their common ethnic qualities and manners, they appear so similar that often people forget that they are individuals. Each one of them is working in his or her own way to define his or her position on the new stage.

For three years in America, Tran, Paw, Cham, and Sy have led a very isolated life. They have not felt part of school life and do not know how to become part of it. Because they speak broken English and know little about their new culture, they are separated from the others. As Khleif (1978) states, "Language becomes, by definition, the chief marker of boundaries" (p. 159). "An ingroup cannot be understood apart from an outgroup; both are interlocked into a unity of opposition; one cannot be understood except in terms of the other" (p. 163). Awareness of the situation of students on the boundary not only enables us to help them integrate into the mainstream culture, it also helps us understand ourselves. School is the place for these youngsters to have their first experience of their new culture. Therefore their schooling should prepare them to become part of the culture, not only by teaching them the language they need, but also by helping them understand the world they live in.

On the last day of the school year, all the students gather in the cafeteria for a school assembly. The students seat themselves at tables, each table crowded with at least two dozen students. The hall is filled with sounds of loud laughing, talking, clapping, teasing, and yelling. At the far back on the left, Paw, Carol, and Lila, a Laotian girl, sit quietly at a table by themselves. Paw sits in her usual way, her head resting on one of her hands and her eyes staring blankly. In the middle, also at the back, Sy and a Laotian boy sit on a bench by themselves. Sy moves his head from side to side, attracted by the loudest noise from the crowd. At the far back row on the right are three boys: Tran, Cham, and a student in a wheelchair. Tran sits there with a constant smile on his face. Cham sits with his body upright, craning his head, trying to see what is going on at the front.

This assembly marks the end of their first three years in American schools. Leaning on the door at the back of the hall, observing each of them, I think to myself: One more year remains for Tran, Cham, and Paw to be in the high school. So far, none of them is sure what to do after that. I wonder whether one more year of high-school education will help them feel more comfortable in their new culture, or whether the culture will remain strange to them. Will they become more sure of their life when they have high-school diplomas? Will each additional year of study build some confidence for Sy? How soon will he figure out his position in life? This day is also my last day of formal research at their school. The picture I have of their sitting literally on the edge of their new culture, trying to make sense of what is going on around them, will remain in my memory forever.

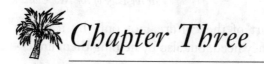

Chapter Three

Tran

Tran likes to tell stories. The first time I met him, he told me that his name, Tran, meant "funny boy." When he was little, he walked with his body swinging from side to side as if one of his legs were shorter than the other. People thought he was funny. That was how he got his name. Among the four of them, he is the only one that can read and write in Lao; of the four, he remembers the most about his schooling in Laos:

> We learned history, math, geography, and Lao in the school. We memorized all the time. Among all the subjects, the math and poetry were the most difficult ones. You get one credit for each of other courses you take, but you can get three credits for math or poetry courses. I took both of them, as I liked challenge

What he remembered the most was not what he memorized at school but what he learned at the Buddhist temple, where he was a monk for seven months:

> That was when I was five. I was a monk in the temple for seven months. In the temple, we studied Buddhism, the Lao history, such as how the country became as what it was today. We read a lot of legends in the Lao culture. I learned that about a hundred years ago, Laos was a much bigger country. The god sent to the Lao a white elephant to help and protect the Lao people and country. But the Thai people and Vietnamese fought with the Lao people for the elephant. They took it away from us. Since then our country became smaller and weaker. We learned a lot of stories like that. Every day we got up between four to five to read.

Later on, when we became better acquainted, he told me a secret:

> Actually I already graduated from high school in Laos, and I had a high school diploma. Nobody knew this at the school here. I grew up with my uncle and aunt, and they were both teachers. So they taught me how to read and write when I was only three. By the time I went to school, I knew everything, so I skipped some grades. I was the youngest among all the high school graduates that year.

Tran told me that his main purpose for attending high school again in America was to learn English. He and his family knew that English would be most important for his success in this country. But ironically, of the four schoolchildren of the family, he was the only one who did not take any English courses during the year I was doing research in their school. Seeing the difficulty Tran was having in speaking, reading, and writing in English, I could not understand why he did not take English, or how he was allowed not to take it. I asked Jane, one of the ESL teachers, about this. She told me that Tran had resisted taking English courses and insisted on taking two high-level math courses instead. After Tran failed geometry "due to his language inability," according to his math teacher, Jane regretted the decision:

> We shouldn't have listened to him and let him do that [refuse to take the English course]. We thought that if we gave him two ESL periods a day, that would cover his English learning, but it turned out we were bogged down by his classroom work because of all the help he needed.

I interviewed Tran several times about this. He said:

> I don't like English course, as you always have to write those book reports. I don't like to write those book reports. You read, then you have to write book reports, always like this. I hate to write those book reports.
>
> I want to learn English, to learn conversational English. I want to speak good and learn more words, not that kind of English in the English class.

> I know my English is not good. I want to improve my English. But I don't think that English class can make my English any better than I take other courses. In other courses, not only I learn English, but other subjects too. I took English in the past two years, now I want to learn something more important.

Tran had listed three reasons for not taking the English course: he did not like to write book reports; he thought the English course could not improve his English as he wished; and he would learn English while studying other subjects rather than learning it as a separate subject. Tran clearly expressed his disappointment with the English courses he had taken earlier and thought they were a waste of time. He preferred to learn English in the context of learning other subjects.

However, with the exception of English teachers, few teachers think that their teaching has anything to do with language learning. Holding the same conventional view, I asked Tran how he could learn to read and write English well if he did not study English. Disagreeing with me, he answered in a loud and definite voice:

> Of course I read and write. I read and write all the time. I read math, science, and do homework with it, that's reading and writing. I live with reading and writing. It should be in here (*pointing at his head*).

Tran did constantly read and write. He read the textbooks every day and did the exercises in them. He read for the assignments and wrote monthly book reports in biology class. He also had reading and writing assignments to do from the ESL rooms. He was busy all the time, yet he seemed never to have enough time for the reading and writing he was assigned. The next sections show how Tran was taught to read and write at the school, and what he was able to do as a reader and a writer.

Reading

Tran liked to read about "great people, real people, and real life." As he said, "I want to learn how they became that great and what they did in their life." But he did not have time to read what he liked; he was too busy reading for school assignments. His everyday reading, his main priority, was to read his textbooks. His second priority was to do the outside reading for his classroom assignments. Last came his reading for ESL work.

"I Can't Read"

The most difficult reading for Tran was his science report, the assignment from biology class. Each month he had to choose an article on science to read and then write a book report on it. This was the reading with which Tran needed the most help from the ESL teacher. At first he would wait until the weekend before the report was due, then he would start to work on it. But because he had so much difficulty with the reading, he found he could not do it quickly on his own. Jane, the ESL teacher, decided to start working with him on the report two weeks ahead of the due date. Usually it would take Tran at least a week to do the reading with Jane's help, and another week to write the report.

Each time, they would go to the library to look for articles on science. For example, once they found three articles. From them, Tran chose one about drugs. Jane wished he had chosen one of the other two articles; one was about pets; the other was about population. Jane told me, "It seems he tends to choose more difficult ones to read. But it's his choice, I can't do anything. I'm afraid that if I told him it was too difficult for him, he would feel insulted." Later on, Tran told me why he chose to read the article on drugs:

> I wanted to know how to grow opium. In my country, there were a lot of opium farms, but I never knew how they do it. But later I found this article is not about growing drugs, but how to stop drugs coming to this country. It is too late. I just have to do it.

This shows a discrepancy between what Tran would have chosen to read and what Jane, his teacher, desired him to read. He chose his reading according to what he wanted to know, while his teacher wanted him to choose what he could handle linguistically. Tran had a dilemma. Literate in his first language (Lao), he was interested in more sophisticated issues and ideas than his limited familiarity with his second language could handle. Because Tran encountered so many new words in the pieces he wanted to read, reading every paragraph was, for him, like cutting beef with a dull knife. He simply could not afford to take the time he needed to do the reading he desired. He had too many assignments to do every day. Very often Tran would start with the reading he was interested in, but because of its difficulty, he would end up switching to topics whose language he could handle but whose content was uninteresting to him. "That is for small children," he would say.

A thirty-five-minute transcript of his reading of the drug article reveals the difficulties he encountered. The following is part of the transcript:

Jane: What does *substantially* mean?

Tran (*giving an embarrassed smile*): You see, I haven't read it. I don't know . . . a lot of words in here. So when I go home, I can't do it.

Jane: That's why I said to you, keep a list of words you don't understand. If you can't tell what it means from the rest of the sentence, bring it in. Because if I don't know what words you can't understand, I can't expect you to read it. In other words, if you don't bring the words in, you're not going to understand the article.

Tran: (*says nothing*).

Jane: Some words you can just figure out what they mean from the rest of the sentence, but some words you can't.

Tran: (*says nothing*).

Jane: Like this one, it's a hard one.

Tran: *Substan*—oh—does it mean *Stand* something?

Jane: No, *Substantially* means—

Tran: *Stand by!*

Jane (*laughs*): No, good guess though. . . . Why do you think it's *stand by*?

Tran: Because "for *substan* . . . ," does it mean . . . something that they want to set up? . . . I don't know what that mean.

Jane: In this sentence, *substantially* refers to how much drugs have been brought down into the United States. Quite a bit.

Tran: Does that mean to slow down?

Jane: The import of drugs into the United States has been slowed down quite a bit. *Substantially* means a solid amount.

Tran: Okay.

Jane: How would you give it back to me? What does the *substantially* mean?

Tran: Does that m— I'm lost.

Jane: Okay, *substantially* refers to how much something has happened. If something has happened in a "substantially" amount, it's a good amount.

Danling: A lot.

Jane: A lot of something. So there is a lot of less drugs has been imported into the United States. Because the U.S. has been giving money to spray the crops. So the crops are not growing. . . . Why has this been successful in Mexico? Why has the United States been working with the Mexicans?

Tran (*reading the article*): Mexican . . . Oh, this part again. I don't know this word.

Jane: *Recognize*. If I recognize you, I know you by seeing you.

Tran: Okay, does it mean . . . ?

Jane: The government understands something . . .

Tran: I see.

Tran gets sidetracked in his reading because of the many words he does not know. Jane ends up spending most of their time together explaining individual words instead of the content. The transcript shows that in a thirty-five-minute period, over thirty minutes were spent on the explanation of individual words and only three or four minutes on the content of the paragraphs. Jane spent seven minutes explaining the one word *substantially*.

Seeing how Tran was reading with Jane, I could understand Tran's difficulties reading the article on his own, and why he disliked reading. He chose to read what he found interesting. But it turned out to be so difficult that he could seldom move on from one paragraph to another without stopping many times. When I worked in a fourth-grade classroom, the teacher said to her students, "When you choose a book to read, open [to] a page. If you find five words you don't know on that page, that means it is too challenging for you. You should choose another one." Tran stumbled on at least five words in each paragraph. Reading what interested him was a challenge. He found he had no control as a reader.

It is easy for us to think that because Tran does not have enough vocabulary, he cannot do sophisticated reading. But that's not the only reason. Goodman and Goodman (1978) studied children from four different nationality groups (Arabic, Navaho, Samoan, and Spanish) as they read in English. They found:

> All of the children, despite limitations in English, were able to read and retell stories. Background knowledge was a significant factor in how well they read and recalled. The more these children knew about the content, the easier it was for them to read and understand the text. (p. 568)

When Tran read the drug article, he did not have any background knowledge on the subject. Both the content and the concepts were foreign to him. He had to rely on the teacher to help him read it. When he read with Jane, Tran was in a passive position. He was either asking questions or being asked them; he was seldom able to contribute anything to the reading. The most frequent phrase he used in the conversation was, "Does that mean . . . ," which reveals the uncertainty of his understanding of the reading and his lack of confidence in himself as a reader. Tran's words at the end of the thirty-five-minute transcript indicate what he understood about himself as a reader after the reading:

> You see, my English is so poor. There are too many words I don't understand. When I read, I might get a little and the most is gone. I don't know what they talk about. So I can't read.

His self-evaluation, "I can't read," helps show why Tran was a reluctant reader. The more reading he did, the more he thought he was "dumb." He was frightened, frustrated, and humiliated by the reading he had to do. He put off reading until he could not delay any more. Simple reading was too childish for him and did not match his interests, but difficult reading highlighted his weaknesses. As a result, Tran avoided reading and remained a poor reader. Tran's reading experiences are similar to what Mike Rose (1989) describes in writing about his own early struggles at school:

> There are times when no matter how hard I tried, I wouldn't get it. I closed the book, feeling stupid to my bones. (p. 57)

> When I tried to read it, I'd ended up rescanning the same sentences over and over, not understanding them, and, finally, slamming the book down on the desk—swearing at this golden boy Johnson and angry with myself. (p. 49)

The reading experience Rose describes presents the point that even native English speakers suffer the same kind of frustration as Tran when they read something too unfamiliar. As Vygotsky (1986) believed, learning happens in areas where learners have already mastered part of the knowledge (p. 86).

When he read with Jane, Tran was not passive all the time. The transcript shows one spark of his thinking, but he did not have a chance to expand or develop his thinking.

Jane: Why are they going to spray it?
Tran: Does that mean . . . to poison this one?
Jane: Right. The United States gave money to a program, so that the airplane can go over the field where the marijuana is growing with the spray, the chemical sprays. Then they can spray the marijuana, and the marijuana plants would die.
Tran: I think . . . that . . . that's not right. The people there can get trouble.
Jane: Who would get in trouble, the people or the government?
Tran: The people in that area.
Jane: That's a real good point. Because that's the problem with spraying chemicals on everything, on any kind of crops that are growing. The chemical is going to the ground and gets

onto the people, right, that's the problem. But in one way it's good. What's been done?

Tran: Nn . . .

Too bad the discussion did not follow Tran's line of thinking, but instead took him right back "on track," to the point of the article. Jane wanted to help Tran get through the reading so that he could move on to the next step: writing the report. Jane noticed Tran's insight, appreciated his thinking, and suggested he put his thoughts in his report. But at that moment she did not have time to build the discussion. Tran's thinking had just begun when it was abruptly ended. Knowing how much their students have to do, the ESL teachers try hard to help them get their work done within the time they have. But because of the rush to get through the reading, answer the questions, and write a report on it, Tran would promptly forget what he had read. As a result, for Tran, reading became simply a job.

"I Have to Read . . . for Her"

Besides helping Tran with his classroom reading assignments, the ESL teachers also assigned Tran some other readings, especially after they noticed his difficulty in speaking, reading, and writing in English. Jane tried hard to find reading that she thought Tran would be interested in, such as novels, stories, and newspaper clippings. But Tran rarely showed any interest in whatever Jane found for him. Once Jane selected the book *Hatchet* for Tran to read. It was a boy's adventure story that Jane thought Tran might enjoy. When Jane showed Tran the book, he took it, flipped the pages with little interest, and said, "Okay, I'll read it." Jane had him read a chapter every day and write about it. The following day Jane would talk with him about what he read.

One incident revealed where Jane's reading stood on Tran's list. One Monday morning, I walked into Jane's room and noticed Tran by himself busy reading *Hatchet* and writing something down from the book. When he saw me, he said, "I didn't get to do this last night. After I did my homework, I watched movies with my brothers. They rented too many movies. I didn't have time to read this. Now I have to read and write for her"—pointing at Jane's seat—"before she comes back from typing something downstairs." Before I could respond, he went right back to his reading and writing. I knew this was his way of telling me not to disturb him with my questions.

A few minutes later Jane walked into the room. When she saw Tran reading *Hatchet*, she asked him, "Did you read it at home last night?" "Yeah," he began, then looked at me, embarrassed, and added, in a very low voice, "Some." He continued to read and write. Three minutes later, he put down his pen, handed the writing to Jane, and said, "Here is my reading." It was the summary of the chapter he had read (see Figure 3–1). The messy handwriting, fragmented sentences, and misspelled words demonstrated his reluctance to do the work. The piece showed carelessness and a lack of effort.

Jane read Tran's writing and was not pleased. She said, "If you would write neater, I could understand you better." Tran stood there, looking relieved because he had finished the assignment on time. Since his writing showed little comprehension, Jane asked him some questions about the chapter. Tran answered the general questions, but faltered on the details. He told Jane that there were many words he did not know in the chapter, and that was why he missed the details. But he did not think the book was difficult for him. He said, "This book was easy, so I put aside, and dealt with the difficult work first. I didn't have time to come back to it, so I didn't spend much time on it." I took this opportunity to ask him a question: "What if we assign you a more difficult book?" "No, no, no," he responded, waving both of his hands and shaking his head hard, but with a big smile. "I don't have time to read those stuff."

Jane was frustrated with Tran's attitude toward reading and started to lecture him about how important it was for him to improve his English through reading and writing. As Jane spoke, Tran said nothing. When she finished, Tran raised his head and asked her, "Can I bring a manual of fixing airplanes

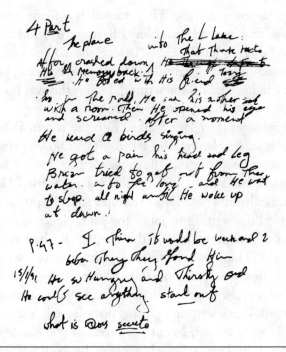

Figure 3–1 Tran's Reading Summary

here, and you teach me how to read it?" Confronted with this unexpected request, Jane paused for a few seconds, then replied that she was not sure she could understand such a manual herself.

Tran's request to read the airplane-repair manual raises a significant question: What is the purpose of reading? In school, Tran read mostly for the teacher or for a grade. His reading assignments required him to write a book report, answer comprehension questions, or write a summary of the reading—all meant to check his reading comprehension. His request suggested that if the purpose of reading was for comprehension, Tran would rather read something that was more related to his life—to his possible future job (he told me that there was a fifty percent chance that he might get a job fixing airplanes after he graduated from high school)— than something that had little relevance. His request implies that he wanted reading to connect somehow with his life rather than reading simply for the sake of understanding words in a text. No doubt the airplane-repair manual would be difficult reading for both Jane and Tran, but because of the significance Tran saw in this reading, he would be more willing to spend time and effort on it. In this case, I believe, Tran would be motivated to accept the challenge. Unfortunately, Tran didn't have a chance to read the manual as he requested.

"Don't Think!"

Another type of reading Tran had to do in the ESL room was to read the ESL textbooks with the teacher in order to practice using English. The following example of Tran reading the ESL textbook and doing the exercises associated with the text is typical of this kind of classroom reading experience.

The setting is Andy's ESL room, small and windowless. In a corner Carl, a Mexican student, is standing on a chair, painting the wall for the credits for his art course. Andy, the ESL tutor, is sitting at the desk. Tran comes in, and Andy asks him:

Andy: How was the math test?
Tran: It was okay.
Andy: You think you did fine?
Tran: I hope so.
Andy: Today, I'd like to do some language exercises with you.
Tran: Okay.
Andy: You are okay with your biology work, right?
Tran: Yeah, but I still have some work to do . . . but that's all right.
Andy: We will have some time for that. Let's do some language exercises first.

Andy opens the ESL textbook, *Turning Point*, to the section on words of possession: *mine, yours, his, hers, theirs,* and *its.* In this section are some advertisements for students to use in practicing possessives. Andy reads the instructions to Tran (see Figure 3–2): "Read the advertisement and write the words that show ownership." Andy asks Tran to get a piece of paper and tells him that they will do the exercises together.

Andy: Read the first picture, Tran.

Tran (*reads*): "Fruit Fizz—Cool, refreshing, different! Serve it on ice. The pleasure is yours."

Andy: Whose pleasure is it?

Tran: I don't understand you, I am lost.

Andy: Look at the ad and answer "Whose pleasure is it?"

Tran: Customer's.

Andy: No, it is in there, in the sentence.

Tran (*Reads the sentence again; then*): It's me.

Andy: No, you don't have to think, the answer is in the sentence.

Tran: It's mine?

Carl (*turning from his painting*): Don't think, just repeat the word in the sentence.

Andy: Yes, don't change anything. Read the sentence again, the answer is there.

Tran (*Reads the sentence again.*): I don't know, I don't understand, I am lost.

Andy: Read the sentence, it's there.

Tran: It's mine?

Carl (*shouting from his chair*): Don't change anything, just say the word in the sentence.

Tran (*frustrated, raising his voice*): I don't understand it!

Andy: Okay, let's start from the very beginning. Read the directions. Here, read here.

Tran (*Reads the directions, then looks up, puzzled, at Andy.*): It's yours?

Andy (*excited*): You got it!

Tran (*shaking his head hard*): I don't know how to do this. I have never done this before.

Andy: Then it's good practice for you. Do the next one, please.

Danling (*interrupting to ask Tran a question*): Would you please tell me why you could not give the answer "Yours" at first?

Tran: Because I thought the ad spoke to me when I read it. So I should say "Mine" or something.

Andy and Tran go on with the rest of the exercise. Tran moves smoothly from one picture to another, until he reads the advertisement with a big smiling female face with the words:

Reading advertisements

1. Read the advertisements and write the words that show ownership. For example, *a. yours.*

Figure 3–2 Tran's Language Exercise

Do you want PERFECT TEETH? Look at mine! I use SOLODENT!

Here, Tran hesitates. He looks at Andy, and when Andy asks, "Whose teeth are they?" Tran responds in a very puzzled tone, "Hers?" Andy shakes his head and says, "No, just read the word there." Tran, still puzzled, reads the word "Mine" and looks at Andy. "Yes, put the word *mine* down on your paper," Andy assures him. Tran writes the word *mine*, but shakes his head hard and, with a confused smile, murmurs, "I don't know."

They move to the next section, called "Locate People and Things." A picture shows a car in front of a camper. Text describes the scene. There are groups of nouns and prepositions in the exercise. Andy asks Tran questions with words and sentence patterns provided in the section. The exercise continues:

Andy: Where is the tent?
Tran: It's behind the tree.
Andy: Where is the family?
Tran: It's in the tent.
Andy: Where is the bear?
Tran: It's in the jungle.

Andy pretends to be shocked by Tran's last answer, and Tran laughs. I then ask, "Have you ever heard about any bears in the jungles?" Tran turns his head to me and says confidently, "No, it doesn't make any sense. But you don't have to make sense, just make a sentence. Don't think!"

Certainly by this time Tran knows how to play this learning game. This episode reveals clearly how language was taught to Tran in a decontextualized way. In these exercises, Tran had to disconnect the language from the meaning and thinking in order to get the "right" answers. His confusion at the beginning was not because he did not know how to read or use the language, but because he was reading for meaning and was trying to do the exercises in the context of real communication. When the text said, "The pleasure is yours," Tran understood it to mean "It's mine." But he was wrong, according to the requirement of the exercise. That was why he was confused. Though he finally learned to read and answer the questions in a detached way—the "right" way—it was still too difficult for him to answer "Mine" when clearly, in the picture, the teeth belonged to the big smiling female face. Though Andy reassured him as he directed him to put "Mine" down as the answer, Tran shook his head as he wrote, murmuring, "I don't know." Tran clearly is reluctant to accept this meaningless way of learning.

As the language exercise progressed, Tran became a confident game player and completed the rest of the exercises smoothly with his teacher. When I challenged his nonsense sentence "The bear is in the jungle," his response showed that he had finally grasped the point: "You don't have to make sense, just make a sentence. Don't think!"

It did not take long for Tran to become a mechanical and passive learner. Powell, Farrar, and Cohen (1985) found that in today's high school, "Passivity rather than intensity predominates" (p. 186) and "substantial numbers of quiet and passive teenagers simply pass through" school (p. 181). They quote a high-school teacher, who said, "Adolescents have been schooled to be passive for most of their lives, and have no idea how to think for themselves, or how to engage themselves in any sort of procedure to find out their strengths and weaknesses" (p. 51). Tran's language exercise certainly demonstrates how our adolescents are trained to become passive learners, and to play school games.

These three examples of how Tran read at school show that he read for the assignment and had little interest in what he was asked to read. He did not have to think, express ideas, or connect the learning with his life; he only had to repeat or retell the texts he read and answer the teachers' context-bound questions. His reading was disconnected and decontextualized, and when he read, he was simply decoding the language symbols of a text.

A Transactional Reading Experience

Tran could express himself and liked to engage in serious thought as long as he was not trapped in comprehension-type reading strategies. I discovered this one day when we read together from *One Thousand and One Nights*. The story was called "Have You Ever Listened to Your Dream Voice?" I was supposed to be tutoring him to read the story. After he had read it, instead of asking him comprehension questions, I told him a story that my father had told me when I was little about why the collection of legends was called *One Thousand and One Nights*:

> In an Arabian country, there was a king who had a beautiful wife. The king loved his wife very much. He liked hunting and often went out hunting for days. Once he went hunting and on the way he found he had forgotten something and came back to the palace to get it. Before he entered the palace, he heard music and dancing inside. He peeked through the crack in the gate and found his wife was having fun with many men surrounding her. He was outraged and killed his wife. Since then he never trusted any women.
>
> Every night he would have a woman sent to him and he would kill her the next day. There were fewer and fewer women left in the country. Finally the official who was responsible for sending women to the king could find no women but his own daughters. If he could not find anyone for the king, he would have to be killed. His older daughter asked her father to let her go to the king, and said to him, "Please send the sister to me before the time I have to go to bed. I will try to let the king not kill me or others." No matter how much her father protested, the daughter insisted.
>
> That night, just before the king and the daughter were ready for bed, the sister came and knocked at the door, calling to her sister, "Please let me in. I can't sleep, as I am used to listening to your stories before I sleep." The king was not happy, but was curious about the stories. They let the younger sister in. The older sister started to tell her story. Her story was so interesting and beautiful, and it lasted until the morning. Even by then she hadn't finished. The king

decided to let the older daughter continue her story. He allowed her to live one more day and the younger sister to return home. That night the younger sister came again with the same request. Because the king had enjoyed the story so much the night before, he let her in and the older sister started another story. Night after night, this continued for one thousand and one nights. The king loved the stories so much that he fell in love with the storyteller. He decided not to kill her and kept her as his permanent wife. Later on, all her stories were collected into the book called *One Thousand and One Nights*.

Tran was fascinated by my story and asked me whether I believed in my own dream voice. I said no, and he then told me a story about how the people in his own country believed in their dream voice:

In Laos, we believe our dream voice. If a person doesn't wake up in his dream walking [sleepwalking], he will die. If he wakes up in his dream walking, he will find treasure. In the past when the French left our country, they tried to take gold out of our country. But they were stopped by the local soldiers. They had a fight. The French escaped without the gold. The soldiers who didn't die buried gold with the bodies of their people that were killed during the fighting, and planned to get the gold later. But the dead people sent the messages home through dreams. Their families and friends went to the place and dug up the gold, but they didn't see any bodies at all. When the French left our country, they buried a lot of treasure, but nobody knew where the treasure was.

I was amused by Tran's story and asked who told it to him. He said that one of his great-grandfather's guards told him. "He told me a lot of stories like that. He is just like one of the family. I like him and miss him a lot. He is still alive and lives in Laos."

Thus Tran and I produced two stories from the one story we read. The oral literature the great-grandfather's guard passed on to Tran lived with him for years, and this story he told me helped me begin to understand the Lao people and culture. We both learned more than one story while we read.

Rosenblatt (1983) holds that reading is an experience of recreating and making meaning through transactions between the reader, the text, and the author. She argues against locating meaning only in the text and seeing the text as a fixed object. She suggests that teachers should lead students primarily "to seek in literature a vital personal experience" (p. 59). In reading "Have You Ever Listened to Your Dream Voice?" Tran and I developed an awareness of each other. He understood that my father liked to tell me stories when I was little, and I understood him to be a good storyteller, and someone who missed an old friend who had told him stories back in Laos. In sharing our stories, we had gained a meaningful experience from the reading. Furthermore, we were able to communicate, to think, to create, and to connect the reading with our personal experience and knowledge.

On another reading occasion, Tran surprised me with his sensitivity and thoughtfulness, a side of him I did not often see. It was in Jane's room, and we were reading some newspaper clippings together about the Iraq War. After the reading, Jane and I began to talk about the previous night's TV news on the war. We talked about the missiles dropping on Iraq. "That country really can stand bombing," Jane said. "See how many missiles dropped on that small land in one second." Listening to Jane's remark, Tran shook his head with a sigh and joined our conversation:

> I am very sad now, sad about Iraq. It's like five big people beating up a small person. It's like a father beating up his son. (*He pointed at the map.*) You see how small Iraq is, how big other five countries, America, German, France, Britain, . . . what is other country, Japan? I don't know, I just feel sad to see five big people beating up a small person, that's like the father beating the son up. That's not fair. Of course America will win, he is too powerful.

Jane and I were silenced by Tran's statements. We looked up at him. He was standing there with his eyebrows tightly knit, and without his usual smile. We did not know whether we were astounded by the unorthodox opinions or simply by the fact that they came from him, the person we thought to be interested only in doing his job and getting good grades for his tests.

Transactional reading-response theorists hold that a text evokes the readers' memories and brings their past experience into their interpretation of and response to the text. Perhaps reading the newspaper clippings about the Desert War might have evoked Tran's memory of his home country: it, too, is a small country, invaded by many bigger countries for centuries and bombed every day during the Vietnam War. Tran's memories and his experience of living through that war helped him feel pain for the Iraqi people. His response was an expression of his feelings and his unique interpretation of the text he was reading.

This time Jane dispensed with comprehension questions and routine language points. Tran's freely offered comments on the war told us more than the fact that he understood the newspaper clippings. He made us think. We had followed the news and voiced our agreements and disagreements with it, but Tran's unique perspective left us speechless. After a few seconds, I asked him whether his father talked about the Iraq War with him. He told me, "This is my own ideas. My father doesn't like to talk to us much."

Unfortunately, Tran seldom had opportunities like this to display or share the deeper side of himself. At school we saw him as being busy every second, trying to finish assignments, shifting from one book to another while flipping the pages. He was too busy to talk, to think, or to read anything in depth. Every time Jane asked him to read something, he would say, "But I have job to do." His favorite word to describe school-work was "job." To him, reading and writing at school was just a job, a chore.

Writing

Tran thought that the ways writing was taught in the Lao and American schools were very different:

> I learned to write poems in Laos, but here they just ask you to write book reports. Writing is different here. Here you write step by step. In Laos, we don't write this way. We write about subject, but not step by step. That's . . . for small people. The smart people don't have to be told step by step. They can get it in the writing. In Laos, we were taught writing has three parts: the beginning, the middle, and the end, then we just write. Here they ask you to write step by step.

Tran's worst experiences in American schools were writing related. Of all the schoolwork he had to do, he spent the least time on writing. He had to write a science book report every month for biology class and a reading report for the geography course, and he also had to write for the ESL teachers. One of the reasons he gave for taking two math courses was, "You don't have to write those book reports for the math class." Tran bluntly expressed his dislike of writing in straightforward language and in his actions. When he wrote, he wrote very rapidly and was messy. After he finished his writing, he seldom reread it. The following sections focus on the contrasts in Tran's writing when he writes out of self-interest and when he writes for assignments.

Writing for Grades

Though Tran managed to avoid taking any formal English classes, he still had to write book reports. He said, "When you take English class, you always have to write those book reports. I hate to write those book reports." Except for math and music, every other class required them. His biology class required the most frequent book reports.

The first day I was in Jane's room, she showed me Tran's first monthly science report and told me, "This doesn't represent his writing. He's mainly copied the article he read. His writing is much lower than that." I read the report. The vocabulary and the sentence structure showed that Jane was right. I was not surprised, as even native-speaking English students copy materials for reports.

I had a chat with Tran about his understanding of book report writing. The following was our conversation:

> Danling: What do you understand a book report is?
> Tran (*looking very confused*): What? Me understand?
> Danling: What should you do in a book report?
> Tran (*still confused*): This . . . is . . . about the rising of the temperature. . . .
> Danling: I mean what your teacher usually asks you to do in a book report?
> Tran: Something about the story you read, something important from the story.
> Danling: Do you write your own opinions of the reading?
> Tran (*confused again*): My?
> Danling: I mean what you think of the story. In other words, do you write if you like the story you read or not in your book report?
> Tran: No, no, I just write what is in the story, but not what is not.

Tran took a piece of paper out of his bag and handed it to me. It was the requirement sheet of the book report that the teacher had given Tran. "Step by step," in Tran's words, it showed how to write the report:

Page one: Cover page (6 points)
Title of article, author(s), source, date, page article may be found, your name.

Page two (5 points)
One-page summary of the article in your own words (What is this about).

Page three: Review of the article (6 points)
Your opinion of the topic covered (3 points):
• Did you find it interesting?
• Did you learn a new concept, an idea?
• Did you expand your knowledge?
• Was it worth reading?

- Would you recommend it to others?

Support your opinion.

Quality of article (3 points):
- Was it well written? Why?
- Was it clear, that is, did you understand it?
- Did it use too many uncommon words?
- Were there any pictures or graphs to support or explain views?

Support your opinion.

After I read this requirement sheet, I understood very well what Tran meant when he said, "Here you write step by step. That's . . . for small people" (he meant small children). It directed what the students should write on each page, including where their names should go. I knew that the teacher's intention was to help the students organize their writing. She was giving them the form and the structure. What remained for the students to do was, in Newkirk's words, "to give short answers or fill in big blanks" (1991, p. 332). But Tran did not appreciate these directions, however well-intentioned they may have been. Instead, he felt insulted.

Tran did not follow the directions for his first monthly book report. After reading the requirement sheet, I said to him, "You didn't do 'Page one.'" He looked at it and said, "Wow. . . . But too late. I am done." I then pointed to the instructions for page three and said, "You didn't do this part, either." He read the directions for page three, moved his finger from one line to another, turned to me, and said, "They are in it." He went on:

> You don't have to say it, it is already in the writing. I wrote about it, that's what I learned. I read it, that must be interesting. I talked about it, that's to recommend it to others. Why should I say it? When people read it, they can tell. It's already in it. I don't have to say it.

After saying this, he put his report back in his folder and said to me, "Anyway, it's finished, it's done." I understood his meaning perfectly: in summarizing the text he showed what he had learned from the reading. There was no need to repeat it again. The fact that he did the reading meant that he found it interesting to read, and the fact that he wrote the report was his recommendation to others. The requirements for the book report were implied in his writing. He did not think that he had to say it again.

However, a week later, Tran got his report back, graded C for his failure to follow the specific instructions for page one and page three. Since that first book report, every time Tran would work on a science report, he would check the requirement sheet and answer the questions one by one. The following was a typical "page three" piece from Tran:

MY OPINION OF THE TOPIC COVERED

This article have a lot interesting information about inviromental get concerned by burning and spill oils. I learned new thing about oil spill and burning oil. I learned how smoke from oil burning to get enemy planes and satellites system confused.

I think this article was worth reading. I would recommend this article to other people.

QUALITY OF ARTICLE

This article is well written. The ideas were clear. There were many new words but I use the dictionary. There were 2 pictures and no graphs.

Every sentence was like an answer to a yes-or-no question: Is this article worth reading? Yes, I think this article was worth reading. Is this article well written? Yes, this article is well written. In writing his so-called opinions, Tran did not go beyond saying more than yes or no. Tran's book report contains a typical feature of student writing: it does not have self-involvement. It shows "the emptiness of 'dry runs' in school writing" (Britton et al. 1975, p. 14).

Even though Tran initially failed to write the required review because he thought the requested material was implied in his summary, he eventually did so for the sake of grades. Since his first report, he seldom expressed much of an opinion about the book report writing; he just followed the teacher's directions. Consequently, his grades went up. He received nothing lower than B or A- from then on, although he continued simply to copy words, phrases, and sentence structure from the articles on which he based his book reports.

The rise of Tran's grades from C to B or A- did not mean that he had become a better thinker or writer, but rather that he had learned to follow directions more obediently; in fact, he had become a less self-controlled learner. Furthermore, he would write more to please the teacher and obtain a good grade than to please himself. Unfortunately, this type of book report writing was the main genre used for the writing assignments in Tran's classes. As Applebee, Langer, and Mullis (1987) reported from a survey conducted by the National Assessment of Educational Progress, report writing covers eighty percent of writing that high school students do in schools.

No Time to Write His Stories

In the ESL room, Tran had a greater variety of writing. Besides writing reports about his reading, Jane and Andy would ask Tran to write stories or personal narratives. Once Jane and Tran read an adventure story together. Following that, Jane asked him to write a real adventure from his own experience. Tran became quite excited about it and quickly responded, "I had too many adventures in my life. I know what I want to write about it. My escape, my escape from Laos to the refugee camp."

The next day I helped Tran write his adventure. I asked him to tell me the story first. He pointed at Laos on the wall map and started:

> Tran: From here, we escape, we walk, in the dark, in the rain. We can't walk during the day, there are a lot of soldiers, Lao soldiers and Vietnamese soldiers. They hide in the jungle, in the mountain, and here in the town too. We had to take a hard road to escape.

Danling: Did your family escape together?

Tran: No, I escaped with Sy. My brothers and sisters escaped earlier, and from different way. Cham and Paw escaped together. From there (*pointing at the northern part of the country*), across the Mekong River. When we escaped, we couldn't go that way any more. A lot of soldiers there. We took the way here (*pointing at the southern part*). It was much more difficult way. There were . . . some . . . I don't know how to say in English, some animals, that would eat people in the jungle and mountains, not wolves, but something like that. We had to be very careful.

Danling: Only two of you escaped?

Tran: No, there were twenty-four people together, and three leaders. My cousin was one of them. They came from Thailand and knew the way, so they helped us to escape. The leaders had guns. One walked ahead to check the road safe or not, and we hid in the cave. If it was safe, then we would go. One leader walked in the middle, another walked at the back. We walked in the dark, can't make any noise. But too many people, walking on the leaves, tza . . . tza . . . making a lot of noise. We were nervous, very nervous.

Danling: Did you know other people in the group?

Tran: No, only my cousin. In our group, we had a general's family. They were the most important people. If something happened, we others would die first. The leaders would protect them first. Because they paid more. Each person paid three thousand *baht* (Thai money), but general's family, they paid twenty thousand *baht* for each. Sy and I didn't pay as much as others as my cousin was one of the leaders. The general and his wife were old and sick. The leaders had to carry them all the time in the jungle, up and down, they couldn't walk at all. It was very hard to walk, in the rain, in the dark, walking in the water. We were so tired. We carried our clothes, food, and some . . . what do you say in English, something, you can use . . . to pay people.

Danling: Money?

Tran: No, not money, something worthy a lot of money. No, not gold, some treasure, we could pay people in case something happen. Everybody had all their things on their back. We had ours too. We were so tired. We were afraid, it was so easy to get lost in the dark. We were so tired, so weak, and hungry. We want water. A lot of time we didn't think we could make it.

Danling: How old were you?

Tran: I was eleven and Sy was six. We got on the boat and crossed the Mekong River at the dark. The light was searching on the river, and there were pirates too. We just missed their boat when we got across the river. When we got to the Thailand, that doesn't mean we were safe. There were a lot of bad police on the border. They know we tried to escape, they took our money or treasure away from us. They asked for pass, a kind of green pass. The people didn't have the pass, they had to sing songs in Thai. Sy and I were too young, we didn't have to do anything. Many girls got raped and sold to the opium farms by the bad people there. Sy and I were almost sold to the farms. Two policemen who checked us, one wanted to sell us to the farm, the other was a good one, he said, "No, you can't do that." So we didn't get sold. We lost each other on the border, then we found each other about an hour later. That was scary. After we crossed the border, there was a long way to get to the camp. It was not safe, a lot of bad people tried to rob us.

Danling: Do you remember the date when you escaped?

Tran: Yes, October 25, 1984, a Friday. That night Sy and I drove to my cousin's house. No, we didn't drive, we took car, the car you can rent. Yes, taxi, took taxi, to my cousin's house. Then we took a boat to the jungle and walked into a small house there. We saw twenty other people there. They would escape too. We had . . .

Danling: Whoops, we ran out of time. Would you please write down what you told me at home? Let's see, you first mention the date when you escaped, how old you and Sy were, and the route you took. Then tell the happenings on the way—how dangerous, how fearful, and how tired you were. You've just told me a very interesting story, you have to write that down. You just write everything down first, we will work on it more. Okay?

I was sorry I had to stop him. I wished that I could just let him talk. Tran had so much to say and got so involved in telling his own story. Usually he would check his watch and ask for permission to do something for his next class. But this time he just talked and talked. His English flowed easily, and he took charge, expressing himself in his own words. I was fascinated by everything he said. I had read some stories about how boat people escaped from Vietnam, but this was the first time I listened to a person who had actually experienced such an escape tell his own story. I learned things that I had never thought of before. I wanted to know more. Tran must have more stories. I thought that writing would give him a chance to tell his as-yet untold stories.

The next time I saw Tran, he showed me his draft. It was very short. I could tell he had tried very hard, as there were four beginnings on the two pages he handed to me. I read his draft and told him what it was I wanted to know more about. He took the draft back and agreed to write more.

Two days later when I met him again, he gave me what he had written. It was still quite brief compared to what he had told me. I offered to help him work more on it, at least to help him finish writing what he had already told me. But he shook his head and refused my help:

> No, I don't like other to help me to write. Not because I don't like you, but I can't write when others help me. I would be so lazy, just let you do it. If I have to write, I like to write by myself, without others tell me this or that. I have a lot of work, other jobs too. I don't have time to work on it. I'm sorry, that's done.

It was a shame, but I understood. Writing in a second language is not easy, and the lack of time made writing even more difficult for Tran. He had tried hard this time. He knew he had a lot to say, but there was too much other work to deal with. He only had enough time to keep up with his assigned schoolwork; he could not afford to take too much extra time to work on this piece of writing. To finish! To get it done! That was how he survived in school. He had a lot of stories to tell, but he was too busy to tell them.

I thought that if Tran could write out his escape story, how much he would benefit from his own writing: he could relive his past experience at a distance or in a different way; he could express what was buried in his heart; he could learn to speak and write through writing; he could understand his past and look at his present differently. And his readers would gain as well. People who read his story would be educated. They would not only get to know Tran and the people who had shared his experience, but they would also appreciate more of what they have in the United States today. Thus, Tran's writing would touch not only Tran's heart and head but the others' too. It was a shame that he had no time to write his story because he had so many "jobs" to do—jobs that disconnected and alienated him from himself and others, from his past and his present, and that kept him positioned on the edge of his new culture.

"I Want to Sing My Own Songs"

Though Tran experienced equal frustrations in his reading and writing, there was a difference in Tran's reading and writing experiences. When he read, he diagnosed himself as a poor or "dumb" reader; but when he wrote, he seldom criticized himself that way, although he had a lot of difficulty in writing. Instead, he would say, "I can write well if I have more time." He was a more confident writer than he was a reader. But seeing how Tran rushed through his work every day, I doubted I would ever get a piece of his writing that would demonstrate real pride.

From September to March, Tran wrote many book reports for the classroom and some assignments from the ESL rooms, but nothing on his own. However, he never stopped expressing his wish to learn to write songs. Each time he came back from his music class, he would say with a shake of his head, "That's not what I want. I thought I would learn to write songs in that class." One day in April, he wrote a song on his own and showed it to Jane and me.

Blue Girl

Blue Eye Girl
You are so lovely
   with you standing there
I'm so aware of how much I care
   for you
You are more than now
You are for always
I can see you in my dreams
   come true
Don't you ever go away
You make me feel this
There's nothing I can do
And when I see you
I only want to say I know you
Oh! blue girl
The song U bring me
Every day and every night
   see U in my mind.
How I've waited for that day
Some time I wonder
U'd ever come my way.

Jane and I were excited by Tran's poem and asked him what inspired him to write this beautiful verse. He smiled and said, "That's kind of thing I always want to write. In our country, we often sing to each other to express what we feel. I like to write poetry and songs to express what I feel. I learned to write them in the Lao school." He told me that he hoped that someone would help him put his words to music, because "I like to sing my own songs."

Tran expressed a lot of personal feelings in his poem. He had told me earlier that he liked girls with blue eyes, and he wished he could have a blue-eyed girlfriend. His personal feelings were connected to his cultural tradition ("We often sing to each other to express what we feel") and molded by his past experience ("I learned to write them in the Lao school"). In his writing, Tran linked his past with his present experiences and so connected his two cultures. When he wrote from his heart, he found the right words to express himself. More important, he enjoyed writing songs and wanted to write more.

In June, before school was over for the year, in the midst of final exams, Tran wrote another poem:

I love-U-Mom

I didn't mean to tell you
I didn't mean to go far away from you
So U have to understand, Mom, I love you
The word Mom, It's still always in my mind
Mom isn't just a word
Mom can be good or bad
but always in my mind
Mom, it's very important to me
Mom, can be a teacher to her child
Mom, can be a good wife to her husband
Mom, can be a housewife who cares for a family
Mom, can be everything for a female
So, Goodbye, Mom, Mom.
Please pray for me
When I see the sun rise up in the morning
I think of your face
When I was young, every time I was down
You built me up and taught me right from wrong
Even though, I was the black sheep of the family
You still care about me
Mom, mom, I would missing U
And I always love you, Mom!

Knowing Tran and especially having heard some stories about his childhood from a daughter of a close friend of his family, I was touched by this poem. Tran's biological father had deserted his family. His biological mother brought up Tran and his two sisters alone. Right now, however, she is not in this country. Tran lives with his adoptive parents. Tran's poem expresses his love and longing for the mother he wants to be with. Tran's poems and songs prove that he can write beautiful pieces. When he is allowed to write what he really wants, he can find the time and the words for it. After writing "I love-U-

Mom," he took it to Jane and asked her to help him polish his language. He told me he would like to write more poems like this.

There are distinctive differences not only in the quality of Tran's book report and poetry writing, but also in the way Tran wrote and felt about the two types of work. In his poetry, he followed the rhythm of his passion ("Oh! blue girl/The song U bring me/Every day and Every night . . ."); but in his book reports, he followed the rules of the teacher ("This article is well written. The ideas were clear . . ."). He treated book report writing as a job: to get it done and get the grade. Whenever we asked about his book report writing, he would only mention his grade ("Oh, I got a B+"). But when he wrote his poetry, he would proudly show it to us, enthusiastically read it to us, and tell us that he wanted to make his poems into songs ("I like to sing my own songs"). Certainly Tran was more in control of his poetry, in terms of content and language, than of his regular school assignments. The language of his poetry was fluent and rich; he made few grammatical errors, and his writing flowed smoothly. By contrast, the language and sentence structure of his book report writing were copies of those in the teacher's guidelines. With broken and incoherent sentences ("This article have a lot interesting information about invriomental get concerned by burning and spill oils"), his book reports were dry and empty.

Tran was a substandard reader and writer when he had no control over his writing and reading, or when he read and wrote simply for the grades and teachers. But he could show himself to be an insightful thinker, a compelling storyteller, and a passionate poet when given the chance to read and write to express his own ideas and emotions. Unfortunately, his endless schoolwork seldom gave Tran any time—or even allowed him—to express what was deep inside him. Instead, he was forced to follow the rules and directions of others. His schoolwork constantly reminded him of what he could not do, while his own writing and the stories he told me prove that he was more literate and had a higher potential to succeed in his new culture than his schoolwork showed.

Chapter Four

Paw

Paw, at sixteen, was a very shy, quiet girl. When Jane first introduced me to her, Paw gave me a very faint smile through her long hair, which hid half her face. Her eyes were cast down to avoid direct contact with me. At that moment I could not have guessed that we would eventually become so close that we could share our experiences in the new culture, our memories of the past, and our feelings as women caught between two cultures.

A Real Reader and Writer

Paw enjoyed reading and writing more than anything else in her life. When she finished her schoolwork and housework, she would sit in her room reading or writing by herself while her brothers and sister would watch TV, go to the malls, or play outside. On weekends and holidays, her family would usually visit relatives or friends or go shopping. Paw would prefer to stay at home, doing schoolwork or reading and writing for herself. She told me that those were the moments she enjoyed the most. With nine people in the house, she seldom had time to herself. So when the family went somewhere, Paw would stay at home to savor the peace and quiet of the deserted household. "It was so good, nobody, no noise, and nothing would bother me while I was doing my own things. I usually do my schoolwork first, then I would read and write for myself."

Paw could not read or write in her native language, though

she had had three years of education in a Lao school. She thought that was because

> we didn't learn to read or write in the Lao school, but just learned words. I never read a story in the Lao school, but memorized words there. Now I forgot them all, and can't read or write in Lao.

So Paw was mostly illiterate before she started school in the United States. She learned many Buddhist stories from her great-grandmother, whom she was very close to: "We talked all the time, and she taught me a lot of things." In the refugee camp she started to learn English. There she went to Sunday school and studied the Bible. She believed this experience helped her become a Christian:

> You know, I think I know more about Christian than Buddhism, because I never read any books about Buddhism, but I read the Bible. I read the Bible as stories. It is like the stories that my great-grandma told me to teach the morals to the people and teach us how to live. I don't read the Bible as God's words. It is the stories told by people, not by God.

When Paw reads, she constantly connects her reading today with what she already knows. When she read the Bible, she connected its teachings with what she knew about Buddhism. Her past experience is important to her, and she would never depart from it:

> I have double religion, a Buddhist and a Christian. I learned about Buddhism from my great-grandma, and about Jesus at the camp. I will never forget what my great-grandma told me, and I will always be a Buddhist. That was what I told my great-grandma before I left my country.

Toward the end of her second year of study in America, Paw became a more fluent reader and writer, and her interest in reading began to grow. Besides reading for schoolwork, she borrowed books from the library. Later, she started to buy books on her own with the money she made from her summer job and put aside for college. She told me:

You know, I seldom buy any clothes. They are too expensive. I want to save my money for my college. The only thing I wouldn't mind spending money on is books. I love books. It feels so good that I can read books, read stories on my own now. In the past I could only listen to the others.

One day when I was at her house, she showed me all the books she had purchased. They were almost the only books in her house besides the ones she and her brothers brought from school. The titles were varied: *Love Is Fire, Rachel Lindsay, Just a Summer Girl, Flowers for Algernon, Emily Climbs, Catherine George, Honeymoon House, Julie of the Wolves, Point of Lost Souls.* She told me, "I love to read classics of romance and adventures." When her brothers would tease her, saying, "You only like to read love stories," she would argue back, "No, that is about people and life." Her reading list reflected her interest in "ordinary people and their everyday life," in contrast to Tran, who liked to learn about "great people and their great life."

When the ESL teachers would mention a certain book, Paw would ask them to loan the book to her, and she would read it when she did not have much schoolwork. Sometimes after reading one such book, she would get excited and share her reaction to it with the ESL teachers. Once I heard her say to Jane, "I really like the book. I cried when I read the ending. I wish that girl would go with the man that she loved so much." It was very rare to hear Paw talking about something with so much feeling; her voice was louder than usual, and full of emotion.

Paw had been a student in the high school in Riverside for three years now. She felt she was a literate person because she could read and write in English. She was not a social person and had few friends. Books became her faithful companions. Whenever she had time, she would read and write; as she put it, "I read to understand others and write to understand myself."

The ESL teachers knew that Paw liked to read, so they often recommended books to her and gave her books as gifts. She appreciated the gifts, but she would often say with a sigh,

> I wish I could have more time to read these books. I have so much homework and housework. I wish I could have more time to read the books I like. I'll just have to wait until the vacation comes. Then I can have some time to read.

When I asked her some questions about reading—What did you learn from reading those books? Why do you like to read those books? What is the difference between reading for assignments and reading for your own pleasure?—she answered:

> What I learned the most from those books was that the people should trust each other, especially the people who love each other. If they don't trust each other, they don't have happiness. You know, my mom and my father separated for twelve years, because they trust each other, so they can happily live together today. I love to read those books because I like to know about the ordinary people and their life.
>
> When I read for the teacher's assignment, I have to read the books she asks us, no matter whether I like it or not. When I read, I have to remember the things in the book, otherwise I can't do the test. When I read on my own, I just read and enjoy it, I don't have to worry about anything.

Paw's interest in reading reflected her down-to-earth personality. As mentioned earlier, Paw was different from her brothers. The three brothers dreamed of having a rich life in their new world, but Paw wanted "to have a good family, a person who can care for me and love me." There was a connection between her personal interest and her reading preferences and, in turn, her reading reinforced her life values—"people should trust each other." Obviously there was a difference between the reading she did for pleasure and the reading that was required for school. When Paw read for pleasure, she connected real-life experience with what she learned from the books—"My mom and my father separated for twelve years, because they trust each other, so they can live happily today"; when she read for school, she had tests on her mind—"I have to remember the things in the book, otherwise I can't do the test."

Paw liked to write, too. She told me that she kept a diary:

I like to write. Especially when I am depressed, or angry, or when I am very happy or very sad, I would write to let my feelings or emotion out. It was like talking to some close friends, I can just pour my heart out without worrying about anything. No matter what I say, it won't hurt anybody. I love to write. My diary is very private, nobody knows I am writing, nobody can read anything there. That is me, and I don't let anybody read it or even touch it.

I was pleasantly surprised to find that she was writing on her own in this way and thought it would be a rare opportunity to read her diary. At the same time, I knew that a diary was a very private thing. One day when we were talking in the kitchen at her home, Paw suddenly left the room, and soon came back with a silk-covered notebook in her hand. She told me that this was her diary. She turned to a page and said to me, "You can read this piece." I was surprised and felt privileged and flattered. It was a poem about herself. I remember a few lines:

I am a moody teenager,
just like anybody else around.
Sometimes I am high, and
sometimes I am down,
sometimes I am happy, and
sometimes I am so depressed. . . .

Whenever I think of myself,
I laugh myself to death . . .

This poem, a self-portrait, opened my eyes and gave me new insight into Paw. In school, she impressed me as a quiet, hard worker and an insulated young adult. In her poem, I could almost hear her laugh aloud, and see her jump up and down, a relaxed, typical teenager. In her writing, Paw had a chance to relax and be what she could not be in life.

I read the poem at least three times, trying to remember as much of it as possible. When she saw that I was interested, she turned to another piece. She read it herself first, then handed it to me, saying, "You can read this, too." It was about how she missed a boy she liked in the refugee camp. Now he was in Canada, and they could not see each other. The piece was full of emotion; in it, Paw recalled how happy she and her friend were as they played together in the camp; "those unforgetful days will always be in my memory and only in the memory. Now he is there and I am here, can't see and can't talk, but just think of the days when we were together."

I did not know what I could say after I read the piece. I knew that Paw was a very private person and seldom shared anything like this with anyone, including her family. After a long pause I asked, "You don't have any contact with him?" "Sometimes he would call me," she replied, her eyes downcast, "but I never call or write to him. In my culture, girls are not supposed to call the boys or do anything first." This helped me understand further why writing was so important to Paw. It was the way for her to express her feelings and ideas openly and candidly; it was a way she could be true to herself.

This sharing was a turning point in our relationship. Once she shared her diary with me, we became closer and closer. We often shared our stories, our excitement and frustration. When I conversed with her, rarely did I think of myself as being triple her age. Despite the difference in our age and experience, our sharing brought us together as equal conversational partners.

I asked Paw when she had started her diary and how long she had been writing it. She replied:

> Last year, when the ESL teacher asked us to write a journal in her class, she said we could write anything we wanted. So I wrote a lot and became interested in writing. Since then I've kept a diary for myself and whenever I have something, I will just write. It is like talking to a friend. I really love it.

I was glad to hear that her diary writing was a continuation of her school writing. Jane was also happy to learn that Paw was writing on her own at home. She expressed the regret that she could not have her students write as they did last year:

Last year, I asked them to keep a journal. They would write any-thing they wanted to, and I would be the only person who would read it. I asked them not to care about spelling or grammar, just write. Everybody wrote. Paw wrote the most and wrote some things that were very personal, such as how she felt when she was at the school, things like that. But now they are main-streamed and have too much work, and don't have time to do anything like this.

From her very first day in the American school, Paw real-ized how important it was to learn English well, and she made up her mind that she would try her best. In her first written piece about her new experience here, she wrote:

The first day at school I was afraid because I didn't know how to speak or write so I went to many different classes and I real-ized that English was the one that I must study hard and do my best, because English was my favorite subject even though I know it will be hard for me to do so, but I knew myself that I tried my best and I do the best I can do.

After that day, I was very happy that I was able to write and read a bit of English and I hope that one day my English will be getting better and better.

I love to read because reading was one thing that can improve my English. I always kept one thing in my mind was I must do my best and be responsible for what it had to be done.

The rest of this chapter describes how Paw did try her best to learn to read and write in her English classes, and how dif-ferently she was required to read and write in her intermedi-ate (A level) and lower-level (B level) English classes.

Start with a Joy and End with a Loss: The A Level Class

Last year, in the tenth grade, Paw was in a self-contained ESL class. She did well in all her subjects, especially English. This year, she was mainstreamed and assigned to the intermediate (A level) English class. She worked hard to keep up.

For the first couple of months in the A level English class, she read, wrote, and did the same assignments as her peers. It was not easy for her, but she "enjoyed studying together with the American students and learning the same things with them." She especially enjoyed the writing.

Her first writing assignment was to write about "your personal experience." The teacher asked the class to make their own choices. They could write about the people they knew, the places they visited, and the experiences they had. "Make a list of things that you did, and then circle the ones you want to write about," the teacher told the class. Here is Paw's list:

People	*Place*	*Experience*
Manichan	Thailand	Volleyball
Joe Smith	Lao	Illness
Janet P	Canada	English
Kim Dennis	Boston	Come to America
Linda	Connecticut	

She circled "Come to America" and wrote about it for her first week's writing. During the second week, she wrote a second piece about her experience in Thailand. This is the piece:

THAILAND

Thailand is one of the countries I have live in. I lived there for three years. Thailand is not a big country, but they have about 100,000 to 5,000,000 people living there. Most people there farm for living.

My culture and Thai culture are similar. For example: the way we talk, write, religions, beliefs, living, and customs. Thai live under the rule of the king and Queen, but my country lives under the rule of the Communist.

My family and I ascaped from my country because my dad was a pilot before the communist ruled my country. The communist threw you in the work camp and brain washed, if you connected or had been working with old government. This happened to my father.

In Laos we had to do what the government told us to do. If you go against them they may kill you or throw you in jail. So we decided that the only way that we will have a better life is to escaped.

We escaped to Thailand. In Thailand we went to a refugee camp called Napho. It was not a big camp but many people from other countries lived in that camp. There were 9 parts all together in the camp, and most people lived in a group. For example, if you are Vietnamese, you had to live in your part, which means you had to live with your people.

In the camp some people had a job, but most people didn't have jobs, because there were too many people and the system was very small. They needed only a few people to work at the camp.

Some jobs people did were filling out forms, cleaning, translating and more. People who worked there didn't get payed. It was a rule but they had a bonus for the people who worked for. For example: if you worked there y would get more food and other things they give out to the people more than a person that didn't work.

It was very hard to lived there. We slept in a small hut and we had to get a water from a well and had to boiled before drinking it. There was not much food and many people got sick and some were died. Things were too expensive to buy.

In 1988 we got a sponsor (my uncle in Mass.) and we allowed to come to United States.

She told me that she enjoyed writing about her experiences: "That's the kind of writing I really like to do. I have a lot to tell and to say. If I could, I would like to write about my great-grandma in the next piece. I really missed her a lot. Now she is dead. She died last year in Laos. I was very close to her."

Unfortunately, in the second month of the school year, the writing assignments were directed away from the personal and toward more text-bound essays or compositions. They were more restrictive, topic-controlled assignments than the earlier ones. For instance, after the class read a story written by Edgar Allen Poe, they were asked to write a mystery scene or something that produced frightening feelings. Paw wrote this short piece:

ADVENTURE ENGLISH
FOR COMPOSITION

One night in winter, soundless night in the house, my family
were out to eat, I was alone in the small room doing homework. The wind were browing the cool air though, it made
myself felt like my heart beating faster and the clock ran so
slow. three later, the sounded of Feet step were coming directly from the front door, suddenly it open, meanwhile my heart
almost stopped beating. But after I saw a person who was coming in, it made me felt free, because it was my mom.

Compared to the personal stories Paw wrote during the first two
weeks, this piece was more "for composition" than personal
expression. But she was able to bring her personal experience
into it: "It was a true feeling. I had that kind of feeling all the
time. But it was not a true story. Maybe it was, I couldn't remember it." This was the last piece of the four that I collected of
Paw's writing in the A level class during the first six weeks of
school. Later, Paw began to have more and more problems with
the reading assignments. The writing became more focused on
the students' answering questions at the end of the text.

Paw's textbook was an anthology of American literature,
and the selections within it were compiled chronologically. It
was very difficult reading for Paw, especially the earlier sections, because the language, style of writing, history, and concepts implicit in them were unfamiliar to her. As a result, Paw
needed a lot of help with her English reading. Whenever I
was in the ESL room, Jane let me help Paw with her reading,
thinking that I had more background in literature than she
did. The first selection Paw had to read was a speech given by
Patrick Henry in the eighteenth century. The speech called
for the American people to awaken in order to free themselves
from British control. It expressed strong opinions and beliefs.
The style was argumentative. When Paw came to me, she
asked me to help her answer the questions at the back of the
text. One question was: "What made this speech so effective?"
It called for an answer that pointed out the repetitions,
rhetorical questions, and figures of speech in the text.

Paw did not understand the terms *repetitions, rhetorical,* and *figure of speech.* When I tried to explain these to her, she became lost and confused. So I went into the text and pointed out the repetitions, the rhetorical questions, and the figures of speech to her. She did not ask me any questions, but simply copied down what I pointed out to her as the answers to the questions. I asked, "Do you understand those terms now?"

She shrugged without saying anything or looking at me. I asked again, "Do you understand this text? This is a really difficult one, even for me."

She answered me very softly, "A little bit, but not much."

"Do you think we should go over the text together?"

"No, I don't have time. I have to turn in this assignment today," she answered.

So, with my help, Paw did the assignment without much understanding of the reading and turned in the work on time. But what did the work mean to her, or to the teacher? The exercise was to help the reader see how the text was constructed and what made the speech effective. Paw did not understand the content or the historical period, so she had a difficult time discussing its construction. It was as if she was expected to analyze why a cake was good before she had even tasted it.

Paw's English teacher realized that Paw was having more and more difficulties. She simply did not know how to help her:

> I could tell in the class, Paw couldn't understand me. And our reading didn't interest her either. One day when we watched the videotape, Poe's "The Fall of the House of Usher," I saw that she had such a hard time. She turned her face aside and had a very bitter expression on her face. I didn't know what I should do. Should I ask her to leave the room or what? I just didn't know what I should do. She didn't participate in any class activities either. One day I divided boys and girls into two groups to have a debate. But she simply left her seat and sat in the corner doing her math. In a situation like this I just don't know what I should do.

In November, two months into the school year, Paw's English class went on to read about the Enlightenment. The following terms from the reading were discussed in the class: *Transcendentalism, Romanticism, realism, industrialization,* and *Western exploration.* In her homework, Paw was expected to explain these terms in her own words. She came to me for help. Looking at those terms, and knowing that we only had half an hour to do the work, I knew we were facing a difficult task.

"Okay, let's do *Transcendentalism* first," I said to Paw. She opened the hard-covered two-inch-thick textbook to where this term was defined through speeches by Emerson, articles by Thoreau, and poetry by Whitman. I knew that we did not have time to go through all the readings. I wanted to find a shortcut to help Paw get through the work. I hoped that somewhere I could find one or two paragraphs in the text that explained the general concept of Transcendentalism. I read the introduction to these authors, trying to find paragraphs that would elucidate the term. Realizing that I had to go through Emerson's speeches, Thoreau's articles, or Whitman's poems, I was overwhelmed. I very quickly scanned one of Emerson's speeches, and found that the concept of Transcendentalism was not explained in one or two paragraphs but permeated the entire speech. There was no shortcut. But since we did not have enough time to read the texts, what should we do? I thought of E. D. Hirsch's dictionary of cultural literacy, which stood on the windowsill covered with dust. I was so happy to see that dictionary at that moment; I thought that Hirsch's American cultural encyclopedia would surely help us get this job done. But to my surprise and disappointment, I could not find the word *Transcendentalism.* Finally I gave up and, turning to Paw, I asked, "What did your teacher tell you about Transcendentalism?" "She said it was to do yourself," Paw answered. "Anything more than that?" I asked her. She shook her head and said very softly, without looking at me, "I don't know." Only ten minutes were left. She did not have one term done. I felt I had no other choice but to tell her my own understanding of Transcendentalism. Paw practically copied my words one by one on her worksheet: Transcendentalism—to rely on yourself, to trust your own voice, to break away from

the old tradition. I wanted to further explain to her its historical significance and its effect on the present American spirit,
but there was no time. We had other terms to do.

After Paw left the room with the work we had done, I felt
guilty for giving her the answers, and frustrated by the impossible task of trying to help Paw achieve any significant learning. This time I, too, had been entrapped by the system—to
get the work done for its own sake. I knew that the experience
Paw and I had gone through was not rewarding to either one
of us. Nor was I helping her to study; she had not learned anything from the exercise. We had cheated! I felt terrible, and
Paw was depressed. Before she left, she told me sadly, "I wish
I didn't need this kind of help, but I couldn't do it on my own.
There was too much for me to do."

Mike Rose's (1989) discussion of one student's reading
describes Paw's situation:

> Certain elements of his [the author's] argument, particular
> assumptions and allusions, were foreign to her—or, more pre-
> cisely, a frame of mind or tradition or set of assumptions that
> was represented by a single word, phrase, or allusion was
> either unknown to her or clashed dramatically with frames of
> mind and traditions of her own. (p. 182)

Paw was unable to identify with her textbook's western
assumptions and concepts. The abstractions made no sense to
her. Her English teacher was aware of Paw's problems with
the assignments and was frustrated, too.

> I could tell Paw had more and more problems with the texts
> now, especially when we got to the abstract material. Every
> day she looked so depressed. She simply was not getting any-
> thing. When we studied Longfellow, I explained his poem
> stanza by stanza. I could tell that Paw still didn't understand.
> But I didn't know what I should do with her. I have so many
> students, and I can't give all my time to her.

We were all short of time. Paw did not have enough time
to learn; her English teacher and I did not have enough time

to help her. We all felt guilty and frustrated. Within two weeks, Paw decided she could not handle it any more. She went to tell her English teacher about her frustration. The teacher suggested three choices and asked her to choose one as the solution to her problems: she could have someone in the class tutor her; she could be given different reading and writing assignments; or she could move down to the B level. Paw took the third choice, as she did not want to be singled out in her present class. She stated, "I want to do the same as the others in the class."

It was not an easy decision for Paw to make. It meant a lot to her to study at a higher level. She had worked very hard in the A level English class. Her English teacher did not want to send her to the B level class, but she thought that Paw set "too unrealistic" goals for herself:

> You know she could stay in my class if she could accept B– or C for her work. But she wanted A's. How could I give an A when I saw so many grammatical mistakes and incorrect sentence structures in her work? I knew she had difficulty with her reading and work, but when I asked her to do lesser assignments, she refused. She wanted to do the same things with the class. I appreciated her efforts but think she set unrealistic goals for herself. I think she'd be better off to move down to the B level if she pushes for A's all the time.

The way the teacher wanted to solve Paw's problems was to give her easier assignments, but Paw refused. She felt humiliated and separated from her peers in this way. She said to me several times, "I just want to do the same as the others. I wouldn't feel good if I did something easier than the others. I know I need help, but I can't help it, as I have too much work." The English teacher's solution reflects a common practice in American schools: when we find our students cannot read or write well, we let them read or write less rather than find another way to help them learn—"lower the expectations" and "water down the curriculum" (Oakes 1985; Powell, Farrar, and Cohen 1985). Paw needed help, but she did not want to learn less. Her teacher's solution was a rejection, when what Paw was looking for was an invitation. Mike Rose (1989) has suggested a better way to help students on the boundary like Paw, by describing his own learning experience:

> Nothing is more exclusive than the academic club: its language is highbrow, it has fancy badges, and it worships tradition. It limits itself to a few participants who prefer to talk to each other. What Father Albertson did was bring us inside the circle, nudging us out into the chatter, always just behind us, whispering to try this step, then this one, encouraging us to feel the moves for ourselves. (p. 59)

Should Paw read this paragraph, I think she would say that that was just what she had hoped her teacher would offer; instead she was offered the option of less and easier work in the class.

Study for Tests and Write for Grades: The B Level Class

In early December, Paw was transferred to the B level English class, the lowest track. When she started her work in the B level class, she was given a different reading assignment from the others. She was asked to read a western story called *Shane*, while the rest of her class (except Cham, her brother) read *Huckleberry Finn*. Paw looked very unhappy every day for quite a while; she became even quieter than before. Looking at her obvious unhappiness, Jane and I became worried. Paw did not want to talk about why she was so depressed. When we asked, she would just sigh deeply and shake her head. When we tried to verbalize for her—"Is it that you don't like the teacher or the students there?"—she would say, "No, the teacher and the students are nice there." "Then why do you look so unhappy? Can we do anything to help you?" Jane asked in a very worried voice. Paw tried to sound casual: "I am fine, I just miss my old class. I like my old English class better."

Paw's former English teacher was surprised to learn that Paw missed her class and was unhappy in her new placement. She said, "I thought she would be relieved and happier, because the work should be easier and it was her choice to move down." Though I could not get Paw to express what exactly made her so unhappy, Jane and I thought that she must have been suffering from very low self-esteem. As Oakes (1985) put it, "Not only has track position been directly related to self-esteem, with lower-track students scoring lowest on self-esteem measures, but placement in lower tracks has been shown to have a corroding effect on students' self-esteem" (p. 148). Instead of feeling relieved, as her former teacher had expected, Paw felt heavy and humiliated, even more when she found she was separated out again, once she was in the lower class, by being given a different reading assignment. Her desire to do well and to fit in went unrewarded. She was more marginalized than ever.

The curriculum in the B class was very different from that of the A class. Of the five school days each week, three were spent on vocabulary and two on reading and writing. As the teacher in this class said, "These students are low and really need skills." Every Friday there was a quiz on vocabulary, and every month there was a test on reading. A typical weekly schedule of assignments follows.

Mon:	READ "Maren's Escape" and "The Arrest"
Tues:	VOCABULARY DEFINITIONS #24
	write vocabulary test 22–24
Wed:	Study spelling and vocabulary
	write misspelled spelling word 5x
Thurs:	READ "Smuttynose" "The Trial" pp. 25–38
	& do notes
Fri:	ST # 24 VOC MASTERY TEST 22–24
	STUDY STUDY STUDY
	Note: COMPLETE "Moonlight Murder on Smuttynose"

HAVE A GOOD VACATION

The weekly schedule and the three capitalized words "STUDY STUDY STUDY" sent a clear message to the students about what the teacher cared about most: vocabulary and tests. The teacher told me that the vocabulary sheet she used for this eleventh-grade class was "from a ninth-grade nationwide spelling list."

Unlike the students in the A level class, the B class did not read from an anthology. They read stories and novels the teacher chose for them. She said, "I choose books for them which I think they can handle." Once the reading assignment was a novel called *The Ox-Bow Incident*. The following is a conversation that Jane had with Paw about the book.

Jane: What did you do yesterday, Paw?
Paw: I read *The Ox-Bow Incident*. But I read a couple of pages, then I put it down. I just couldn't read it. I don't like it at all.
Jane: I read it a little too. It was awful. I couldn't go on reading it, either.
Paw: *Shane* was better, though I didn't like it either. It was much better than this one. I simply couldn't read this one. I have to stop all the time. When I read a book I liked, I could read it for hours without stopping until I finished it. But for this one, I couldn't do that.
Jane: I wonder why she chose this book for you to read. Do you choose your own books to read?
Paw: No, never. She just asked us to read, and we had to read.

It was not that the language or the concepts in the story were too difficult for Paw; it was simply that the content itself was not interesting to her. She could not engage in the reading. She did it because it was assigned by the teacher. Detached as she was from the content, it was a struggle for Paw to keep reading.

After the reading, the teacher would give a quiz to check the students' comprehension. Here is an example of the monthly reading quiz:

WALTER VAN TILBURG CLARK: *THE OX-BOW INCIDENT*
READING QUIZ: CHAPTER TWO, PP. 64–94

Directions: This is an open book test. Answer the following questions in complete sentences. Include specific details from the text.

1. Who is Sparks? Why does he decide to go with the "posse"?

2. Who is Ma Grier? How does she feel about going?

3. Who is Tetley? What position does he take?

4. What information convinces everyone that they should form a posse and go after the rustlers/murderers?

From the questions, we see that the quiz simply entails text recall and requires a large amount of memorization. It does not provoke thinking or provide for any connection between the text and the real-life experiences of the students.

Usually Paw did not have any problems doing the text-recall kind of quiz; she was a careful reader and could remember very well. But these quizzes were only a very small portion of her assignments for English. She spent most of her time on vocabulary and spelling. Sometimes she used the time in her other classes to work on her spelling exercises. Once she said to me:

> Today I was doing my English vocabulary in the science class. The teacher found out that. He must be mad at me. The kids were chatting and I had nothing to do. So I took out my vocabulary sheet to work. I was so embarrassed when the teacher came to me and saw what I was doing. I am going to have vocabulary test today, so . . .

Every Friday Paw had a vocabulary test. These tests were on her mind all the time. The English teacher had a very fixed and specific way for her students to learn vocabulary:

Step 1: Circle the words that will be tested.

Step 2: Find the definition of each word in the dictionary and copy it down.

Step 3: Use the content of the reading to make sentences with the circled vocabulary words.

Step 4: Have a weekly vocabulary test.

Paw did not have any problems with Steps 1 and 2, but she ran into trouble with Steps 3 and 4. In Step 3, the teacher tried to connect the new vocabulary words with the reading by asking students to make vocabulary-word sentences based on the reading. In this way, she felt, the students would both learn the new words and show their understanding of what they read.

Paw needed much help in writing the sentences required in Step 3. Usually Jane or I would make a sentence with the word to show her how to use the word, then Paw would make a sentence with the word relating to the reading. For example, for the word *convenience*, I wrote:

You can come to my house any time at your convenience.

Paw wrote:

It's Mike's convenience to kill his brother.

For the word *definite*, I wrote:

Please give me a definite answer about his visit.

Paw wrote:

To a definite, Mike killed his brother.

From the sentences Paw made I could see the root of her difficulty. While she could spell the new vocabulary words, she had no idea how to apply them in a context that was so remote to her. In addition, she had little enthusiasm for creating sentences with words she seldom read or heard or would expect to use again. (While helping her with her sentences, I became stuck myself once when we came across a word with which I was unacquainted.)

I could tell that Paw was not really learning the language. I had to help her reconstruct each sentence. For example, we changed "It's Mike's convenience to kill his brother" to "Mike killed his brother at his convenience," which was still awkward. I tried to tell Paw how to use this word more meaningfully, but she did not show much interest and just did what I told her. After we finished the sentences, she gave the work to her English teacher. She then returned to the ESL room and began working on her spelling test.

The last step in the four-step process, and the critical one for supposedly demonstrating vocabulary acquisition, was the quiz. Paw took these quizzes very seriously: "I want to do well and get a good grade." I frequently heard her saying, "I have to work on my vocabulary for the Friday test." She was always the last one to turn in her quiz. She seldom was able to finish the test within a class period, so she often asked to continue the test in the ESL room.

The vocabulary test usually had three parts: dictation, multiple-choice items on synonyms or antonyms, and fill-in-the-blanks. For example, for the first part, dictation, the teacher would read a piece that contained the words from the vocabulary list, such as the following (the italicized words are the words from the vocabulary list):

New *Process College*
Academic Circle
Occurrence, NM 42507

Dear *Professor* Smart:
    With *reference* to your *correspondence* about *salary* increases for *seniors*: your *proposal* is *completely* retarded. Has it *occurred* to you what *catastrophes* will *occur* if we *admit* your policy is *changeable*? We will have referees at the *admitted* gate of every *procession*.
    I *propose* you drop this crazy idea.

Very truly yours

The teacher would dictate this text to the class and then have the students underline the vocabulary words and sign their name at the end. This example shows how the teacher tried to create a context for the words she wanted her students to master. She tried very hard to include all nineteen words from the vocabulary list in this short text. "I stayed up until midnight in order to make this test," she said. But the short letter the teacher wrote was too artificial to serve as a context for these vocabulary words. From the very beginning (the address, "New Process College, Academic Circle, Occurrence, NM") to the end (the signature of the student), it's clear that the content was artificially created as a meaningless vehicle for a list of unrelated words.

In order to prove my point, I could replace those vocabulary words with Chinese words. See if the content of the following letter provides any context for the recognition and reinforcement of the new words. (Actually I do not have to use Chinese words; any nonsense symbols will do.)

New *Chen Xu Xue Yuan*
Xue Su Circle
Chu Xian, NM 42507

Dear *Jiao Shou Smart*:
   With *Gen Ju* to your *lai han* about *gong shi* increases for *lao nian ren*: your *jian yi* is *che tou che wei de* retarded. Has it *xiang ji* to you what *bu ke chi shi de jie ju* will *chu xian* if we *ren ke* your policy is *ke jie shou de*? We will have referees at the *ru kou* gate of every *guo dao*.
   I *jian yi* you drop this crazy idea.

                                        Very truly yours

If this text makes little sense to us, then it is enough to say that this kind of exercise provides no context for students to learn vocabulary, but instead just presents them with a bunch of decontextualized sentences.

   In addition to the fact that the text was nonsensical, the intent or tone of the letter, I think, would be offensive to Paw's cultural values. Paw's father told me, "I teach my kids to respect the old, to care for others, and help each other." Paw would probably not argue against "salary increases for seniors" or write to a professor proposing "you drop this crazy idea." When Paw signed her name at the end of the letter, I could imagine how detached and disconnected she was from the act. As she said, "I got it right just by listening to the

words, but I don't know what it meant." When she showed
Jane the dictated letter, Jane was so upset that she came to me
and said, "I just have to show you this. It doesn't make sense
to me. How can she [Paw's English teacher] ask them to do
this?"

But the dictation was only a portion of the vocabulary test.
The following are some typical examples from part two, a
multiple-choice section called "Synonyms in context" (students were asked to "select the best definition"):

1. The President *conferred* honors upon the soldier.
    a. bring together for discussion
    b. consulted
    c. bestowed upon
    d. talked about

2. Crime is not *confined* to the cities.
    a. to keep indoors
    b. legally restricted
    c. to keep within designated limits
    d. liberated

Paw usually had the most difficulty with this part of the
test, because she did not understand the choices. For
instance, in the first example, she did not know the meanings
of some of the lettered choices: in the first item, she was confused by the choices *consulted* and *bestowed upon*; in the second,
she was unfamiliar with *legally restricted, to keep within desig-
nated limits*, and *liberated*. How could she make a best choice
from a field of unknowns? When she continued her test in
the ESL room, Jane would explain what each choice meant.
After Jane's explanations, Paw was able to answer the test
questions. But when she did this part of the test on her own
back in English class, it was like a game of chance for her.
The success of the work depended more on chance than on
real ability in English.

The last part of the test consisted of fill-in-the-blank items.
The instructions were, "Write the word in its correct form."
The test looked like this:

Recently, history books have given _____ to life on the _____ in the early 1800's. It was not one of _____. The early settlers were under a lot of _____ to obtain the meager _____ they needed to survive. People were _____ to their homes when bad wind storms _____, there were few places they could _____ for meetings to _____ with one another, and the _____ metals that were discovered soon "panned" out.

prevail   pressure   prairie   assemble   substance   precious
splendor   consideration   confer   confine/confinement

Paw had memorized the vocabulary words out of context. In this part, she had to insert them into a strange context that had no validity to her. She could not know which words rightfully belonged where, let alone decide the proper form each should take in the sentences. Take the two words *confine* and *confinement*, for example. She had learned the definitions of these two words from the dictionary, but she did not know them in context. Thus, she could not tell the difference in the usage of the two words. I saw her shifting back and forth between *confine* and *confinement* as she took the test. First she put one in one blank, then she erased it and replaced it with the other. Then she erased again and put the first one back. She repeated this putting-in-and-taking-out action again and again, six times. Finally she wrote down words without thinking, because she ran out of time. Very often she left the classroom looking dismayed, with her work unfinished.

With Jane's help, Paw was managing to get good grades. The English teacher was not happy about this, but she had to grade Paw according to the number of "right" answers she had. One night the English teacher called Jane to complain. The two teachers had an argument on the phone. Jane got very upset and angry, and told me about it afterwards:

> She [Paw's English teacher] was very upset with me and said that I didn't tell the truth about Paw's ability. She thinks Paw has very low skills and is in a sublevel to her class. Every time when Paw takes the test, she needs more time and has help

from me. She [the teacher] thinks that Paw is cheating and this is not fair to the others. She claims that once Paw tricked her and took her test home. I told her that Paw was too honest to do that. Knowing Paw, I know she had no brain for that.

The English teacher's grounds for complaint on the special treatment given to Paw were legitimate for the normal rules of test taking. Paw did use more time than the others, and she did receive help with her test. In this sense, it might be considered "cheating" and not fair to others in the class. But should we also question the test itself and the way we test our students, instead of just blaming the test takers? Frank Smith (1986) defined educational testing as "the opposite of the way people behave, learn and are evaluated in the club" and called it "discrimination against the confused" (p.142).

The vocabulary and spelling worksheets covered about seventy percent of the work the students did in the B level English class. Paw stated, "In this class we don't write. We just do vocabulary and spelling. When I was in the other English class, the teacher asked us to write about our life experience. I really like that."

During the seven months of Paw's study in the English B level class, I collected two essays that she wrote. In the B level class, the writing was more form-controlled and text-bound than in the A level. The students had to do a worksheet before they started the actual writing. The following is a sample of the worksheet before the writing.

IRENE HUNT: *No Promises in the Wind*
ESSAY: JOSH

Directions: Complete this sheet before you write your essay.

I. NOTES: Josh is,

Character:
good
bad

How and why did he become separated from his family?

Reasons he was able to survive:

Events and people who brought about his change of character:

II. OUTLINE

Topic sentence (This must state the whole idea of his character)

Details (one paragraph each)
1.
2.
3.

III. CONCLUSION/SUMMARY

In the low-level class, the students were considered to "really need a lot of help with their writing. They need to be told what should be put in the writing and how to organize the writing," according to the teacher. This worksheet exercise was to help students form their ideas and organize their writing. It was intended to help students work on the necessary parts of what should be in an essay. Then, when they wrote, they should knit those ready-made pieces together. In the A level class, Paw did not have to do this preliminary exercise before writing. Now, in the lower level, she had to learn the form before she could begin to write.

How Paw learned to write a topic sentence is a good example of this step-by-step, guided way. The first sentence Paw wrote for the "topic sentence" of the Josh essay was the following:

Josh left his family to survive during depression because he thought he was right and other people were wrong. But at the end he learned everybody could make a mistake. He learned how to care about other people and he also learned to forgive.

The comments Paw got back from the teacher were as follows:

It's too long as a topic sentence. It should be like this:

Josh left home because he thought he was right and other people were wrong.

Please try it again.

Paw reasoned that since the worksheet instruction said, "This must state the whole idea of his character," she should include enough information about Josh to communicate his character, but it was too difficult for her to do in one sentence. That was why she wrote three sentences instead. Now she had to try again, while taking care to avoid using the teacher's sample sentence, although the teacher's sentence contained parts of Paw's original. Paw worked at this difficult task for three days. The second time, she wrote it like this:

Josh left home feeling sure he was right but through hard experiences he finally learned how to forgive people's mistakes.

She went back to the English teacher with this version, but again it was not approved. Paw went to Jane to ask for her help. Together, they worked out a sentence like this:

Josh Grandowske, was an angry 15 years old who left his family during depression to try to survive on his own.

The English teacher was still not happy, so Paw wrote a fourth sentence:

Josh, 15 years old, left his family to survive during the depression because he thought he was right and other people were wrong.

This time, the English teacher said it was okay and told Paw to begin her essay. The first sentence in the essay ended up as the following:

When Josh is fifteen years old, he leaves his family because he believes he is right and other people are wrong.

Paw's five opening sentences were not much different from one another, except that some included a bit more information than others. She was shifting the same words back and forth and trying to fit them into a pattern that only the teacher knew. It was as if Paw was putting a puzzle together, but the whole picture or design was only in the teacher's mind. For three days, Paw's frustration and confusion grew. The teacher's notion of a topic sentence remained a mystery to Paw (and also to Jane, who said, "I just don't know what she [the English teacher] wanted").

We knew Paw would work as hard on her "Josh" essay as she had on the topic sentence. In the end, she received an A for the paper. On it, the teacher wrote, "This is EXCEL-LENT, Paw—Thank you for a splendid paper. I am very proud of you. A P. S. Do watch your verb endings." When Paw showed me the paper, I asked, "Can I make a copy? I will give it back to you tomorrow." She replied, "You can have it. It has no use to me any more."

In contrast to her diary, this "splendid" piece of writing meant little to her. Her diary was a part of her, but this "Josh" essay was just for the teacher and a grade. She would not let anyone touch her diary, let alone read or make copies of it. But she let me keep this piece, her original writing with "splendid" and a big A and the capitalized word "EXCEL-LENT" written on it. Good grades and good comments from the teacher were very important to Paw ("The most exciting thing for me in the school is to get good grades"), but her attitude toward this paper revealed that she felt no ownership of this piece of work.

Paw's learning experiences in two different classes and at different periods have shown a wide variation in achievement in Paw's progression toward the attainment of English literacy. When she was given choices, as she was in the A level English class, she eagerly and openly told stories and expressed her thoughts relating to her past and present life. In the first two months of school, she wrote four pieces, two personal stories, one poem, and a short composition. She demonstrated her engagement in the use of language, using creative thinking and self-expression in her writing. But when choice was denied her, the teacher's expectations became increasingly disconnected from what she knew, and the texts became increasingly abstract, Paw's problems began.

Paw could write well when relating personal experiences. She could read better when relating the reading to a life she knew. The abstract reading and disconnected writing she had to do in class had little to do with Paw's real-world experiences and were totally beyond Paw's ken. Her later experiences in the first English class began to parallel what Adrienne Rich once said: "When someone with the authority of a teacher, say, describes the world and you are not in it, there is a moment of psychic disequilibrium, as if you looked into a mirror and saw nothing" (quoted in Bruner 1990, p. 32).

Paw's experiences in the B level English class parallel what Oakes (1985) found in her research: that there is a distinctive difference in selection of reading materials, classroom and homework requirements, academic expectations, and instructional approaches between high-level and low-level classes. In the low-level class, Paw was confronted with a mechanical way of learning to read and write. She spent most of her time learning vocabulary words from a spelling book, making meaningless sentences, and taking endless tests. From the work I collected of Paw's in the seven months she spent in the B level class, ninety percent was worksheets on vocabulary, reading comprehension, grammar, and sentence structure. In that time, Paw did two and a half writing assignments: two "Josh"-type essays and a paper on fission, which she did for both English and science classes.

Paw was a passionate reader and writer when she could read to understand others' lives and write to understand herself. "When I read a book I like," she said, "I can't put it down for hours." She also told me, "Writing in my diary is like talking to a close friend, you can just let out anything in your mind. But in life I don't really have one I can trust so much." But when she read and wrote simply for grades in the English classes, she suffered through some very frustrating, humiliating, and alienating experiences. Reading abstract material out of context and writing to analyze what made no sense to her was like pounding a message into her head that said, "You just can't read and write."

She had less freedom when she read and wrote in the A level class than when she read and wrote for herself. She had even less control when she tried to learn to read and write in the B level class. In the A class, she first started writing about her life and later had to shift to writing more text-bound essays. She went from a familiar area to an unknown place. It was as if she had left home and got lost in Alice's Wonderland.

When she began in the B level class, she was immediately put into mechanical drills. It was like working on an assembly line in a factory: no speaking, no thinking, no choice, no connection to life and self, just mechanically moving words from the books to the worksheets. Those worksheets isolated her from others and the real world; they froze her thinking and disengaged her from learning.

Paw was a hard worker and a disciplined student. She knew that education was important for her future and that her mastery of English would determine her success in her new world. She studied very hard at school. She believed that school would help her reach her goal of going to college. Unfortunately, her learning experiences in the United States proved to be similar to her learning experiences in Laos, and the words she had used to describe her earlier experience rang true again:

We didn't learn to read and write in the Lao school, but just learned words. . . . Now I forgot them all, and can't read and write in Lao.

In this class [The B level English class], we don't write. We just do vocabulary and spelling.

 # Chapter Five

Cham

Cham had five years of schooling in Laos, but he could not remember anything he learned there. He could not read or write in Lao. When I asked him about his schooling in Laos, he only remembered how he got into the school and how he was punished by his teachers:

> I don't know when I started school in Lao. You know, in our country, if a child could use his right hand to touch his left ear over the top of his head, that means he is old enough to go to school. Maybe when I was five, my uncle, I lived with his family, he took me to school. The teachers asked me to touch my ear over the top of my head, so I did. Then I started school. I was punished all the time by the teachers. Once I didn't do my work, the teacher asked me to stand by the corner on my one leg and with a book on my head. Sometimes he hit my hand with a ruler if I didn't behave well at school. He yelled at me all the time. I really hated school and often skipped the school.

When Cham talked about his past, he often mentioned how he played with his friends: swimming in the river, climbing trees, hunting in the woods, flying kites. Cham was different from Tran and Paw. Tran liked to talk about his glorious school years in Laos as a gifted student and a popular leader among his peers. Paw remembered her great-grandmother, who was her caretaker, mentor, and companion. Cham was outgoing and active—a person who enjoyed nature and activity more than anything else. He fondly remembered the places in Laos he lived, played, and visited. He remembered the palm trees and bamboo that grew around the house; he remembered working with adults in the rice fields and going to the temple, which had a dragon gate. He spoke most often about his life in the refugee camp: its hardships and the adventures he had there. Those were his lasting memories. He wanted to write about them, but he regretted that "I don't have words for them, my English [is] too poor."

Now, in his new culture, he had a very different life pattern. On weekdays, he went to school from 7:10 A.M. to 2:30 P.M. and spent the rest of his time doing homework, watching TV, and helping with housework. On weekends he would go shopping, watch TV, and do housework. Sometimes he would take a walk in the mall with his brothers. During school vacations, he would work with his mother in the factory, packing fish on the assembly line, because he needed to make money to help his family. He said, "In this country, you pay for everything, even play." In contrast to his life in Laos, Cham saw less of the sky and felt less of the presence of nature in his life.

Of the four school-age children in his family, Cham had the greatest difficulty with English. The ESL teacher, Andy, tried to assess his English ability with a test commonly used for the placement of ESL students. The results were not encouraging:

> I was not able to achieve a base. He was too low to establish a norm. Then I tested him with an ESL picture book with vocabulary. I tested him orally. His oral intake was extremely poor. When I write the words, he can recognize them, but can't understand them when I say them to him. Since I had no way to use a common standard to assess his language ability, I had to take a guess. I assume that his written level is four years old, and speaking is under three and a half. He doesn't understand many words. His working vocabulary, or communication ability, is on a four-year-old level.

Consequently, Cham was placed at the lowest level for all his subjects, except art, which did not have a tracking system. He took fewer subjects than Tran and Paw: he had two periods of study hall; one and a half periods for ESL; a period each for English, science, and math; and half a period for art. He studied math two hours a week individually with the math teacher because Cham, as Andy told me, "had problems with understanding the teacher in the class," and he spent another three hours a week on math in the ESL room with Andy. Andy believed that Cham learned better on a one-to-one basis, when the teacher could give him special attention, speak slowly to him, and address his specific problems. Of the courses he took, Cham did best in math. But he did not like math at all. He considered math to be the most useless subject he had to study. Cham decided that science was the most interesting because "you could learn to do things with your hands," but mastery of English was the most important because, through it, he hoped "to get good career and make more money." When I read his report card, I said to him, "You have scored the best in math." He replied: "I wish that was English. I wish I could raise my English score to B or B+. I wish I could improve my English and get an award for ESL. But I know it's too hard. Dreams are hard to come true." Paw observed that "Cham spent most of his time doing the English work at home."

Like his brothers and sister, Cham knew that English was the thing he had to master before he could make any plans for his future in this country. "I want to speak well, learn more words, and write correctly. I want the others to understand me. Then I can learn other things, and get jobs." Unlike Tran and Paw, Cham did not feel a need to do something significant in life, nor did he have a clear-cut goal, such as going to college after high school. He just wanted to be able to get a job that would make good money, whether it be as a mechanic, electronics worker, salesperson, or cook in a restaurant. He said:

> I'd like to work for three or four years, make some money, take a trip back to Laos, then I will see what I can do. I might go to a technical school to learn some skills, to get a better job. I don't want to go to college; that takes too long.

Cham read at home. He was not interested in stories, novels, or poetry. He liked to read magazines and newspapers. He usually spent his study hall time in the library. After he did his homework, he would get a magazine or some newspapers to read. His favorite magazine was *People*. "In that magazine, you can learn a lot about those Hollywood people. I love to read their stories and their life. I love their fancy life." Mostly he would read the classified advertisements section in the newspapers to find a job or to see if something was on sale. He also liked to glance at the movie reviews. When I asked him what he read at home, he answered immediately, "Catalogues, to see what is on sale."

For the first half of the school year, Cham was far behind his classmates in just about all his classes. As stated earlier, because of his difficulties in understanding his teacher, he had to study math one-on-one with the teacher. Cham's heavy accent made it necessary for the science teacher to read Cham's papers for him, while everybody else in the class presented their own. The low level of his reading and writing skills resulted in his reading less difficult books and doing less difficult written assignments from the rest of the English class. His first report card showed:

	Class Work	Final Test
English (B)	D	C–
Algebra (1)	A	B
Science (B)	B	B

With special help from both his classroom and his ESL teachers, Cham received rather good grades for math and science, but not in English. In discussing Cham's performance in English class, his teacher stated, "Even with the D and C–, I graded him more on his effort than on his real ability. According to his real ability, he can barely be placed in high school. I don't understand why they put him in my class."

Cham had the greatest trouble with vocabulary work. Each week his spelling and vocabulary tested poorly. His best efforts might get him seventy percent. Most of the time, thirty percent was the best he could do on a vocabulary test. The English teacher became more and more frustrated with Cham's poor progress and said, "He has such low skills in language. I am a high-school English teacher, and I am supposed to teach literature. I don't know how to deal with this kind of student. He doesn't even have the basic language skills." In the second half of the school year, Cham was transferred from the eleventh-grade to the tenth-grade English B class, the lowest level.

The next sections show how Cham learned to read and write differently in the two English B level classes, and how the different ways of teaching reading and writing affected him as a reader and writer.

"Typically, Cham Would Fail"

Cham's work in eleventh grade got progressively worse. Cham's English teacher complained that Cham should not have been placed in her class and questioned the work the ESL teachers did with him. The ESL teachers felt, in turn, that Cham's English teacher unfairly blamed them and thought that she was the one who should modify her way of teaching and lower her expectations for Cham. Due to this conflict, the director of the ESL program called for a meeting in Jane's room. In attendance were the two ESL teachers, Cham's English teacher, and the director himself. At the meeting, the English teacher was first asked to present her curriculum. The following is an exchange that went on at the meeting between the director of the ESL program and Cham's English teacher:

> Director: Maybe we should start with what your objectives are. Tell me your curriculum.
> Teacher: We have ten words of vocabulary. He [Cham] doesn't look them up, so he doesn't know what they mean. . . .
> Director: I want to know your curriculum. Ten words and what?
> Teacher: They have twenty spellings, plus the different forms of them. They have a vocabulary test every Friday. I expect them to define them and to use them. I expect the other kids to

relate them with the subject, but Cham doesn't have to relate them to the subject.

Director: What do you ask them to do on the test?

Teacher: They have to use them in phrases and sentences. They use multiple choice of definitions in the context and find the words, then write the correct forms in the paragraphs [select the correct words for the blanks]. . . . For them it is a puzzle. It's difficult, I want to push them to use more complicated words. I have to dictate to Cham, word by word, sometimes letter by letter. If I [go] slow enough, he doesn't do badly. Those kids all have poor concentration skills. . . .

Director: What's the next type of test?

Teacher: Literature. About the class reading. The class did *Huckleberry Finn*. That is way beyond Cham. So I did different books with him—*Shane* and *The Man Without a Country*. The vocabulary I gave him was easy too. He has very poor vocabulary. When he read *The Man Without a Country*, he didn't know the words *country* and *sailor*. . . .

Director: What do you expect them to do with the reading?

Teacher: I read aloud to them, go over their notes. But I don't have time with Cham. So I do it with him at lunchtime. I go over the study guide with him, almost everything. I go over questions with him orally. When I read aloud to him, he understands significantly better. I break down the reading, paragraph by paragraph. Cham wouldn't understand the text unless you read aloud to him.

Director: What's the test?

Teacher: It's a reading quiz, quick test: short essay, true or false choice, filling in blanks, and give short answers. Typically, Cham would fail them. . . .

Director: Let's go over your test again. Quiz: essay, filling blanks, identifications, true or false choice.

Teacher: I go over it with them every Thursday. I go over vocabulary and give pretest reviews.

Director: Do you ask them to write something?

Teacher: I expect them to write sentences with the vocabulary. We don't do too much outside writing. I plan to teach them how to fill [out] forms, such as a driver's license, insurance forms, something like that.

The curriculum the English teacher presented stressed vocabulary learning: ten words for vocabulary and twenty additional spelling words plus their different forms each week. Sentence making and weekly tests were the teaching strategies used to help students master those words. The teacher would read the book to the class and go over the notes with the class. The class would then have a test, which required the students to recall the notes they took when the teacher read to them. The writing consisted of creating sentences using the new vocabulary.

We also learned from the teacher that Cham had a lot of problems with his English learning: he failed the tests, did not do homework (looking up the weekly vocabulary in the dictionary), and had very poor comprehension and poor language skills. As the English teacher spoke, she could not stop complaining about Cham's low ability. Each time she did this, the director would interrupt her. In the end, she claimed that Cham's English skills were too limited for him to learn to read and write in her class. "I just don't understand why you placed him in my class," she said

The first day I met Cham in the ESL room, I was asked to help him with his vocabulary worksheet. By working with him, I realized how difficult the work was for him. In my notes, I recorded my impressions that first day with Cham:

This was my first day of working with Cham. I helped him with his vocabulary worksheet. There were ten words on it. He was required first to define their parts of speech; second, to give the definitions; then to make sentences with those words. He looked those words up in the dictionary, and copied down the definitions and the parts of speech. But he didn't understand what *n* or *adj* stood for. I explained this to him, that *n* stood for noun and *adj* for adjective. But it didn't seem to make any sense to him. He nodded his head when I explained to him, but when I asked him, "Do you know what *noun* means?" he shook his head. It was so hard for me to deal with this linguistic issue out of context. The next stumbling block was when we did the definition part. There were several definitions for one word in the dictionary, but should we copy down one or all of them? Cham said, "Just copy the first one down." The most difficult thing we came across was to make sentences with those words. He didn't know how to use them at all. I tried my best to explain how to use each word, but he didn't show any interest and simply copied the sentence that I had written to demonstrate. I was so frustrated to find I didn't know how to help him learn to use those words.

My notes above reflect how Cham typically did his vocabulary work. Because he had to learn the words out of context, he could not remember them or use them, even though he had copied the definitions word by word from the dictionary. Many researchers (Beck, McCaslin, and McKeown 1980; Stahl 1985, 1986; Kameenui, Dixon, and Carnine 1987) have pointed out that word knowledge can hardly be learned out of context. As Baumann and Kameenui (1991) put it:

> When a word is embedded in a rich context of supportive and redundant information, the learner might be more likely to acquire its meaning than when the same word is found in a lean context. In the former context, knowledge of a word is said to be derived, prompted, or assisted by the verbal context (reading or listening). In the latter situation, word knowledge is considered to be unprompted and therefore unassisted by the immediate context. (p. 605)

The way Cham took vocabulary tests demonstrates why students can hardly enlarge their vocabulary by learning it out of context. Take the word *advance*, for example. Cham had copied one of its seven definitions in the dictionary as "to make earlier in time." He made the following sentence with the word: "I advanced my homework last night." Then, he encountered it on the weekly test, in the multiple-choice section:

the *advance* in food prices

a. retrogression
b. make early payment
c. proceed
d. acceleration

He circled "b. make early payment," because it was the choice closest to the definition he had memorized from the dictionary. Further in the test, when filling in the blanks, he put the word *advance* in the blank to create the following sentence: "But they are certain big cars *advance* better."

In all three exercises (making sentences, multiple-choice, and fill-in-the-blanks), Cham was wrong. He made the three mistakes not because he did not do his homework, as his teacher stated, or because he forgot the definition. He made them because he remembered only one out of the seven definitions for the word *advance* in the dictionary, and he had to learn it out of context. Therefore, when he had to make a sentence with it, he used the word in a foreign way: "I advanced my homework last night." The teacher marked it wrong and asked him to correct it as "I did my homework in advance last night." Actually, the teacher's version was awkward too, as most natives would say, "I did my homework earlier last night."

The mistakes Cham made in the multiple-choice and fill-in-the-blanks sections also stem from his memorization of the words out of context. The word *advance*, depending upon the context, can be used as a noun or a verb. When Cham looked it up in the dictionary, he chose to remember it as a verb meaning "to make earlier in time." But the test required him to choose it as a different part of speech, a noun meaning "a rise, especially in price or value." This was the reason for his mistake in the multiple-choice section. Baumann and Kameenui (1991) reported in their recent research on vocabulary instruction, "Some argue that multiple-choice vocabulary tasks 'are useless at best and dangerous at worst' . . . because they are not sensitive to the various dimensions of vocabulary knowledge" (p. 607). Cham's experience with multiple-choice vocabulary tests certainly proves their point. As for the fill-in-the-blanks section of the test, its purpose, in Cham's English teacher's words, was "to push [the students] to use more complicated vocabulary words." But to Cham it was "a puzzle." His inserting the word *advance* where he did ("But they are certain big cars *advance* better") showed that he had not acquired a full understanding of how and when and where *advance* is correctly used.

Of the ten items in the multiple-choice section of the week-ly vocabulary test, Cham got six wrong. And in the fill-in-the-blanks section, he got seven out of nine wrong. As for his few correct choices, Cham said, "I didn't know how I got them right. I got some right by guessing, and some because they were the only words I knew." That was how Cham typically took the test.

Every day Cham did his vocabulary homework, and every week he spent much time studying for the Friday test, which he usually failed. Once, just before the test, when he was in the ESL room, Jane asked him to do a language game with her. Cham usually got excited at the prospect of playing any kind of game. He enjoyed challenges and a variety of activi-ties. But this time he asked, "Can I do my pretest? Today I will have the test." I saw his pretest sheet: twenty spelling words plus their synonyms and antonyms and the rules for capitalization. I asked him whether he had studied them the night before. He said, "I read them and worked on them for a long time last night. They are too hard. I can't remember them. I still don't know them." That day he went to the test with a worried look on his face. No doubt he anticipated another failure.

Cham was also doing poorly on his reading tests. Remember the teacher's complaints that Cham had too little vocabulary to handle the reading: "he didn't know the words *country* and *sailor*" when reading *The Man Without a Country*. True, those words are essential to that story. But if the teacher knew Cham did not have the basic vocabulary to read, then why did she not teach him to learn the words he needed for the reading? Instead, she pushed him to learn even more complicated words in the vocabulary book. Con-sequently, Cham was unable to master the words in the vocabulary book, nor did he have the vocabulary for his read-ing. It was like giving a person who had no clothing dressy suits and silk party dresses, and insisting that these were the essentials for everyday living.

In conjunction with their reading, students had to do worksheets and take a monthly test to check their comprehension. Cham's worksheets and tests were based on separate books from the rest of the class. One book, *Shane*, was a western, approximately a hundred pages in length divided into twelve short chapters. The worksheets and tests I collected for this reading totaled fourteen pages. After every two chapters, Cham had to do a set of worksheets on four areas: setting/time, plot, characterization, and analysis of certain incidents or remarks. With Jane's help, Cham could finish the worksheets on time; but he could not handle the tests.

He took the comprehension test every month. The test had four parts: true or false, multiple choice, fill-in-the-blanks, and a short essay. The first three parts contained one hundred items. They covered almost every detail of the book. When I saw the test I knew I could not handle it. Essentially, the test required Cham to memorize the whole book. As usual, Cham failed the test, getting only one-third of the questions right. Not finishing the test during class time, he took it to the ESL room and continued to work on it there with Jane's help. When Jane saw the test, she was shocked and said, "I read the book, and I certainly couldn't do the test. How could I remember all those details in the book?"

Few of us read to remember everything in a book. We only remember what strikes us as most pertinent in our own lives. Frank Smith (1986), sharing his own reading experience in his discussion on memorization, says, "I would only have to memorize deliberately if I were dealing with something I did not understand—but if that were so I probably wouldn't be reading the report in the first place" (p. 74). The worksheets and tests made reading onerous and difficult, when what should have been fostered was depth of understanding and a lifelong love of reading.

In Cham's English class, little emphasis was placed on writing, except for writing sentences. The teacher had earlier dis-

closed, "We don't do much writing. I ask them to write sentences with those [vocabulary] words." Altogether I collected
three pieces of writing from Cham during his six months in
the class: two short essays and a question-and-answer type of
writing. For each piece Cham needed much help, either from
his English teacher or the ESL teacher, even though writing
was part of the monthly test.

As mentioned in Chapter 4, on Paw, in this B class, the students had to complete worksheets before they wrote. Jane
usually helped Cham do his worksheets. He would first fill in
some information about the characters, the plot, the setting,
and so forth, before he got to the structure of the composition. My notes from a day in December detail this process:

> Jane was helping Cham work on his worksheets for writing the
> essay. Step by step, Jane asked him to put down what he could
> remember about the character he was going to talk about. She
> told him, "You don't have to put them into complete sen-
> tences, just anything you can remember about this character,
> then we can put the ideas into paragraphs."
>
> Soon they came to the topic sentence. Jane said to Cham,
> "Okay, let's do the topic sentence now. Do you know what a
> topic sentence is?" Jane asked him very casually. "Yes, it's
> something, nn . . . that word . . . Oh, yes! It called *details!*"
> Cham was so happy that he had finally remembered the
> expression "the details." Jane was shocked that Cham really
> didn't know what a topic sentence meant. First of all, she
> would have to explain to him what it meant before they could
> work on it. "A topic sentence is the first sentence of your
> essay." Cham nodded his head. "No, that's not enough, it
> should contain all, or should be a summary, of the information
> you are going to talk about." Cham frowned. "It is the first
> sentence that includes a . . . [pause] look at what is put here
> [she reads from the worksheet] 'The topic sentence must state
> the main idea of your paper. (It must embrace the entire con-
> cept.)'" Cham looked down at the worksheet without any
> expression on his face. "Are you clear now? Do you know what
> a topic sentence means?" Jane wanted to make sure that Cham
> understood it before she could help him work on it. Cham
> raised his head from the worksheet and said to Jane, "Can we
> just write it now?" "But I want to make sure you know what it

means, otherwise how can we do something that you don't know? Do you know what a conclusion means?" Cham shook his head. Jane rolled her eyes and slouched down her body and let out a big sigh. Cham kept his eyes on the worksheet with an expressionless face. Jane looked at her watch and realized there were only five minutes left. She said to Cham, "Okay, let me just explain all these terms to you today. I don't think we have any time to write this essay now. We can do it some other time. A conclusion means . . ."

I remember clearly that Jane spent the rest of the period explaining what a conclusion meant. Cham sat there with his eyes on his worksheet, his face expressionless. As soon as the bell rang, he dumped everything into his bag and rushed out of the room. Jane looked at me. We both shook our heads. After a few seconds, Jane remarked, "You see, how can he do the test? He doesn't understand what those terms mean on the worksheet. I still don't know whether he understands what a topic sentence and a conclusion mean after I spent so much time explaining them to him. Am I confusing him?" I could tell Jane was overwhelmed and frustrated. She wanted to help Cham, but it was hard for her to explain those technical composition terms to Cham, who had read and written so rarely and so little.

From Cham's lack of expression and response to Jane, I could tell he was confused and lost. At first I had noticed at least a spark of interaction with Jane, with Cham nodding his head and frowning, eventually he became motionless and stoic. It was too much for him, as well as for Jane. *Topic sentence* and *conclusion* are formal compositional terms. A writer does not have to think of them before starting to write. If a writer has something to say, he or she expresses it. Teachers use those terms for teaching; critics use those terms to analyze writing. But Cham, who had written little in his life, had to deal with those technical terms before being allowed to write. He found himself in the situation that Oakes (1985) described as the usual predicament for students like Cham in American high schools: "Those [low-track] students who seem to need the most appear to be getting the fewest schooling experiences that are likely to promote their learning" (p. 197).

Though Cham had problems understanding the terms *topic sentence* and *conclusion*, he did have a topic sentence and a conclusion inherent in his writing. The following is a short essay he wrote:

> Start Wilson was from Kansas, and he was working for Fletcher. He was going to scare the homesteader so that Fletcher could get their land.
>
> Wilson was an Arrogent man. And he killed Ernie by Challenge and made him mad and Ernie took out the gun and Wilson shot him. After he killed Ernie Wright he scared all the homesteaders. Wilson was a serene person. He was confident and tough man. He thought that no one could beat him. Until Wilson met Shane. Wilson challenged Joe and Shane went to the bar. And got a fight with Wilson, than Wilson was killed by Shane.
>
> In my opinion is Wilson is a bad guy because he thought that money was more important than people's lives.

Though Cham made a lot of mistakes in this short essay, he did show that he knows how to write, in terms of organizing and expressing his ideas. The first paragraph contains a topic sentence, and the last sentence is obviously a conclusion. This essay also exhibits Cham's comprehension of the reading. He understood the main ideas of the book *Shane*.

When he got his essay back from the teacher, it was covered with the teacher's corrections and red marks on the margins and between the lines. There was no grade; the teacher's comment at the end read:

> Cham,
> This needs to be rewritten to put in better order. Please meet w/ me at lunch and we will go over it.
>
> Your details are good—Once the order is logical it will be a good essay. Thank you for all the hard work you put into reading this book. Your good work shows you have made good progress.

At lunchtime, she explained to Cham how to organize a piece of writing. She wrote on a piece of paper:

* *Introduction*
1. Stark Wilson is proud man, killed 3 people, reputation for being fast gunner. . . .
2. Start Wilson was reckless when he accept Fletcher's offer to scare the homesteaders, thought it would be easy, didn't plan on fighting Shane . . .

** *Conclusion*
Ernie—Wilson takes advantage of someone who can not protect himself.

After the teacher had talked to Cham, she asked him to copy his essay in the way she had corrected it. With these instructions, Cham came back to the ESL room. Jane did not understand why the English teacher asked Cham to copy her corrections instead of rewriting it, so she went to the classroom to make sure Cham had not misunderstood the teacher. The English teacher told Jane:

Yes, I did ask him to recopy the paper in the corrected version, because I want him to copy it absolutely grammatically right, to get the habit of patterning, and get the flow, and put the writing in a good order.

Cham copied the teacher's corrected version word-for-word as follows:

Stark Wilson was a gunfighter from Kansas, and he was a tough gunfighter. He was hired by Fletcher to scare the homesteaders so that Fletcher could get their land.

Wilson was an arrogant man (more details). He killed Ernie by challenging him to a gunfighter, first insulting him and made him mad and then Ernie reached for his gun but Wilson shot him before he could even get it out of the holster. After he killed Ernie Wright the homesteaders but Sevett and Shane were scared.

Wilson was a overconfident person. He thought no one could beat him. After Wilson met Shane, he learned a lesson. Wilson challenged Shane to a gunfight and lost. Shane got into a fight with Wilson and Wilson was killed by Shane. In my opinion Wilson is a bad guy because he thought he had the right to take people's lives.

Cham copied it without asking any questions about the teacher's corrections. He assumed that the teacher was right and he was wrong. When I saw that the teacher changed Cham's sentence from "He was working for Fletcher" to "He was hired by Fletcher," I asked, "Do you know the difference between these two sentences?" Cham shook his head and said, "I don't know what was wrong with my sentence, but of course the teacher must be right. She is always right. Maybe she wants me to learn how to use the word *hire.*"

There is a subtle difference between "being hired" and "working for somebody" (I did not know this myself until one day I shared this story with a group of graduate students). So the teacher was technically right in making her correction—somebody "was hired" to kill somebody in the western. But how many Americans know this subtle difference? The teacher did not explain to Cham why it would be better to use "he was hired" instead of "he was working for"; she simply asked him to copy her corrected version. Had this been a learning experience for Cham? I doubt it, especially in light of Cham's comments, "I don't know what's wrong with my sentence," and that the teacher "is always right."

The teacher had made another notable correction on the last sentence of the essay. She changed Cham's opinion from "Wilson is a bad guy because he thought that money was more important than people's lives," to "Wilson is a bad guy because he thought he had the right to take people's lives." Jane and I could not understand why the teacher had to change Cham's opinion by substituting her own, and further, we both believed that Cham's was valid. In the plot of *Shane,* Wilson is a hired killer, so Cham rightfully concluded that he "is a bad guy because he thought that money was more important than people's lives." As was the case with all the other changes the teacher had made to his essay, Cham neither asked questions nor defended his opinion; rather, he passively rewrote the teacher's revision word for word.

When Jane saw Cham's essay covered with red marks and how passively and silently Cham copied the teacher's corrected version, she was worried that Cham's self-confidence had suffered a blow. She also thought that some of the teacher's changes were unnecessary. As a result, Jane decided to have a talk with Cham's English teacher. Their conversation is excerpted below:

> Jane: Can you modify your expectations for Cham? There are just too many red marks on his paper. I think he is overwhelmed by all the mistakes he made. Could we try bit by bit, and not expect him to do everything right at the same time? So as not to give him a feeling that all he makes is mistakes. Let's focus on the important or bigger things first. Let's narrow down, such as looking at capital letters and punctuation this time, then . . .
>
> Teacher: You mean when I have his work, I only look at capital letters, but not sentences, words, or usages?
>
> Jane: Yes, we have to, but not just ignore them, but . . . let's cut down our expectations. . . .
>
> Teacher: I can't understand why he is in the eleventh grade. There is something crazy about the placement. I can't handle the basic skills, just no time for that. When I look at his writing, sentences are not correct, words are not correct, forms are not correct, I have to deal with them. I can't just let them go.
>
> Jane: I mean let's narrow down, focus on a few incorrect things each time, not deal with them all at the same time. I am worried that he is too confused. . . .

Obviously, there was no common ground between Jane and Cham's English teacher. They were talking to each other from different perspectives. Jane wanted the English teacher to be less obsessed with Cham's errors and more encouraging of his efforts. The English teacher saw this as a request to lower her standards, which she was unwilling to do. Their meeting resulted in Cham's transfer in February from the eleventh-grade B level English class to the tenth-grade B level class.

"I Want to Be Like an Eagle"

After six months in the eleventh-grade B level English class, Cham found himself in the tenth-grade B level class. When I asked him what he thought of it, he replied, "I don't know. I can't stay in Mrs H.'s class. The vocabulary is too hard for me there. Mr. B. told me that I can build up my vocabulary in his class too." Unlike his sister, Cham was not bothered by being moved down to a lower grade-level English class. He told Jane that now he had more time because the vocabulary in the tenth-grade class was easier and the teacher did not give the spelling or vocabulary test every week: "That is much easier, we don't have to take the test every Friday. I have more time for other things, not just vocabulary all the time."

In the new class Cham still had to learn vocabulary from the vocabulary book and make sentences with those words. However, there was less pressure now, and he became more talkative and interactive. He spoke more in the ESL room instead of bending his head down to do worksheets or the tests. He participated more in the activities of the ESL rooms, and in school in general. In his new class the reading materials selected were mostly stories from magazines like *Scholastic Scope*. They were mainly about teenage life today. Usually the teacher would read the story with the class, then a discussion would follow. The class had only four students, including Cham. They did few worksheets, but a lot of talking. The teacher was very humorous and tended to make jokes in order to provoke the students to speak and interact in the class. The two American girls in the class interacted with the teacher all the time. Cham spoke little, but he would listen and laugh with the others. He looked much more relaxed than he did in his former English class.

There was no reading test, but there was a monthly writing assignment relating to stories the class read. For instance, after the class read the story "Camikazi Kid," about a boy called Sam who jumped back to the year 1961, the writing assignment was: "Imagine a time in the past or in the future. What did you do or what would you do then?"

That was the first writing assignment Cham received in his new English class. Instead of worrying about the work, he could not wait to write what was in his imagination. He wrote about life in Laos in the year 1912.

> I want to go back in 1912. I want to go back to Laos because that was my old country I was born. How wonderful if I'm going back to Laos. I would like to see how my grand father and mother are doing in that time. The people in 1912 they wear black clothes always when they went to school they were very neat clothes. They studied ten hours a day in the school. In 1912 the people had a small farmily because they didn't had enough food and they didn't had time to take care there family as well. In that time the men were worked hard everyday in the farm. Every two day a week the men had to worked for the government for example they build the houses and dive the lake. The women had strayed home cleane the houses and cooked for the men and took care everything in the house. They live in a cubicle house. Every year the people pay tax to the government like get them rices about two hundred pound. In 1912 they didn't had free to do everything that they wanted to do.

Unlike his earlier writing, Cham enjoyed writing this piece. He did not ask for much help, and he finished in no time. In this piece, he combined what he knew about the life of his grandparents and what he knew about his country. He knew that his grandparents' generation lived a harder life than his parents and had to work much more than his parents did to survive. He knew the people currently under the rule of the Communists in Laos did not have freedom to do what they wanted to do. He wrote what he knew about his country's past and present, no longer struggling to recall the facts from his assigned reading.

In April, he was asked to write on the topic "Spring Fever." At first, Cham did not know what spring fever meant. He looked it up in the dictionary, and still he could not under-stand its meaning. He went to Jane and asked what kind of "disease" spring fever was. Jane replied, "It is not really a dis-ease, but a strong feeling of wanting to go out, do something outdoors instead of working indoors. This happens when the weather starts getting warm after a long, cold winter." After Cham heard Jane's explanation, he almost shouted, "Oh, I cer-tainly have spring fever. I can't wait to go out. I want to climb mountains, to have a picnic on the beach, go sailing, swim in the ocean, play volleyball." As he wrote, he kept saying, "Oh, I forgot to put ——— down, that's the thing I really want to do too." Within a single class period, Cham finished his "Spring Fever" composition, in which he wrote about all the things he enjoyed. When he was finished, he read the piece aloud to Jane and me. As he read, he frequently stopped to edit his writing—"Oh, this word is wrong" or "Here, I forget to put *ing*."

Cham's grades improved. He got B and B+ for his two writ-ing assignments. Above all, he enjoyed writing and had fun communicating his own ideas.

The writing assignment in May required him to write on the topic "Why I Want to Be an Eagle." Cham wrote:

> I want to be like an eagle because the eagle is the symbol of freedom in America. The eagle is a bravny fighter. The eagler is a lofty flies [flier] in the sky, and I can fly wherever I want to go, [and] nobody will tell me what I should do or don't. I will be the leader of sky. Perhaps I can fly back to my country in Laos and help my people to have freedom like an eagle. I will protect them, and get them good care. I will teach them to be like the leader of sky. They will become brave people, and always believe in what they can do. Nobady will control them. I will eat fish, quail and snake. I will sleep in a beautiful house with swimming pool.

Cham received an A for this paper. It was the first A he had ever received for his English work. Instead of looking at every mistake, the teacher saw the beautiful ideas in Cham's writing and responded in a very positive way. He bracketed the section "Perhaps I can fly back to my country" to "Nobady will control them" and commented:

> This section is excellent (and touching!) I admire your ability to take your thoughts beyond the ordinary level of the assignment. Very good job w/ this assignment.

In this class, the teacher did not spend a lot of time talking about how to write, or using worksheets to teach techniques of writing. There was little discussion of the structures of writing beforehand. He simply provided the opportunities and the time for his students to write in a self-expressive way. The weekly or monthly tests were replaced by writing assignments that reflected the introspection and self-interest of the teenage authors. Obviously, Cham was benefiting greatly from his new teacher's teaching strategies. He could write now and thought it was fun and exciting.

"I Want to Make a Book to Tell the Stories of My Past Life"

Cham liked to draw. We discovered this after he was placed in the tenth-grade English class. When he was in the eleventh-grade class, he put most of his efforts into English and little on other subjects. His first report card showed a rather low score for art (C–). After he moved to the tenth-grade English class, he began to catch up and catch on in his other subjects. He showed the greatest progress in art. Increasingly, he began to draw on his own.

One day in April he brought in two drawings he had worked on at home. In these drawings Cham had depicted a memory of his home country and an impression of America. His memories were juxtaposed in each drawing. In the first rendering (Figure 5–1), he drew palm trees, a bamboo house, and a river with fish swimming in front of the house. The sun was shining and birds were flying in the sky. In this idyllic

Figure 5–1 Cham's Memory of Laos

scene he had juxtaposed a helicopter, a bomb exploding, and a bus climbing hills. When I asked him to tell me about this picture, he began by pointing to the house in the picture, and saying:

> That was my house in Laos. I remember everything beautiful there, our house, the palm trees, the rice field, the rivers. It was always warm there.

Then, pointing to the helicopter, he continued:

> That was what I knew about America when I was in Laos. I remembered they dropped bombs on our land, the helicopters flying every day in our sky and their buses too.

The second drawing was a variation of the first, with some major alterations (see Figure 5–2). His Laotian home scene still occupied the center space, but it had become smaller, looked farther away, and was overwhelmed by the impression of America, which Cham expressed using bright colors and different shapes. When I asked him to explain this picture, he pointed to the center of the drawing and began:

> This is my country. It will always be in my memory. It is beautiful. It will always there. Someday I want to go back see it.

Then, pointing to all the shapes around the center, he said:

> This all is America. I don't know how to draw about America. It is too much, but I don't really know what it is. That is what I feel about America.

In the first picture, Cham had drawn his country and his impression of America when he was in Laos. In the second picture, he shifted his point of view to America. He drew his old country, Laos, in his memory. It was still in the center, but it had become smaller and less dominating than it was in the first picture. It was surrounded, almost suffocated, by all the different bright red and yellow shapes representing Cham's impression of America.

Cham could not say them with words, but he could show his thoughts through his drawings. Jane, Andy, and I were

Figure 5–2 Cham's Current Impression

impressed not only by Cham's artistic skills, but also by the messages his drawings conveyed. Cham was responsive to our admiration of his work:

> You know what I really like to do, I want to draw a series of pictures about my life in Laos, and in the camp. I want to make a book about it, then after each picture, I will write something to tell about the picture. I want to make a book to tell the stories of my past life.

Jane was delighted to hear his plan. She shared her excitement with the other teachers. Everyone, especially Cham's English and art teachers, were surprised and pleased to hear that Cham had initiated a project on his own. These two teachers and Jane decided to help Cham carry out his project and agreed to give him credits for English, art, and ESL. For the three teachers involved, it was a new and interesting project. As one of them said, "We are just glad to see him want to write [or draw] and like to do it."

Cham started drawing the second week of May. He drew whenever he had time—at home, in study hall, in art class, and in the ESL room. By the beginning of June, I was able to collect a series of fifteen drawings, including drafts. The first depicted a Buddhist temple with a large dragon at the gate (Figures 5–3A and B). Then came a rendering of his house, with bamboo along the side, palm trees at the back, and a rice field close by (Figure 5–4). The next scene (Figure 5–5) was the Mekong River flowing between its banks. Laos was on one side of the river and Thailand was on the opposite side. On the river itself were the refugee boats escaping from Laos to Thailand. Then he drew two pictures of his Lao school (Figure 5–6), showing the Lao flag unfurled on the top of the building. His last two pictures were of the refugee camps in Thailand (Figures 5–7A and B), in one of which (Figure 5–7A) he detailed buildings: the jails, the office, the clinic, the wired fence surrounding the camp, and the trucks for transporting supplies to the refugees.

Two days later, while I was at the school, I encountered a delighted Jane, who burst out:

Temple gate

Figure 5–3A The Buddhist Temple: The Gate

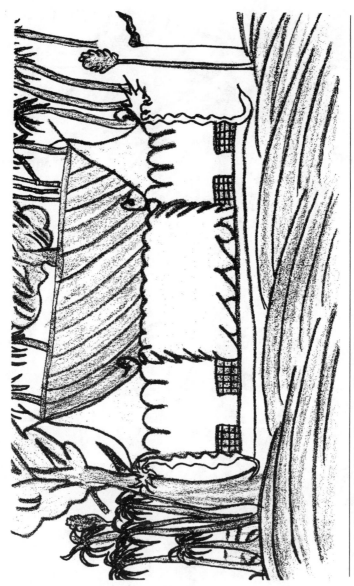

Figure 5–3B The Buddhist Temple: The Back of the Temple

Figure 5–4 Cham's House in Laos

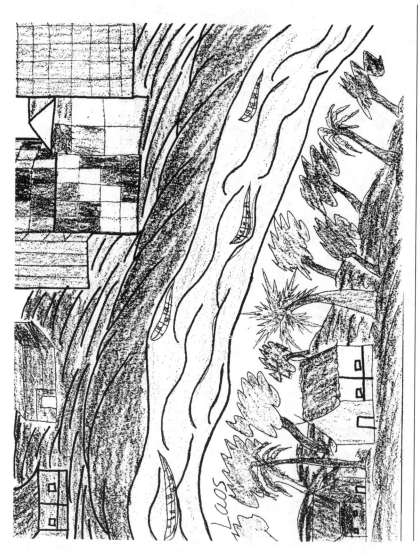

Figure 5–5 The Mekong River

Cham

Figure 5–6 First View of Cham's School in Laos

159

Figure 5–6, cont'd Second View of Cham's School in Laos

Figure 5–7A The Different Camp Buildings at the Thai Refugee Camp

Figure 5–7B Another View of the Thai Refugee Camp

Oh, Danling, you don't know what you missed yesterday, and no one would have believed this before. Yesterday Cham sat here and told us all the stories. He went through one picture after the other telling us all the details of his life in Laos and in the refugee camp. We didn't say anything, nobody said anything during his talk, or even asked any questions. He talked and talked straight, for forty-five minutes, the whole class period. If not for the next class, he would have continued his stories forever. It was so interesting. Having been with them for so long, the first time I heard all this. I really understand my kids better now after all the stories Cham told me.

Jane could not stop telling her story either. Her enthusiasm grew as she told me about Cham and her new knowledge of him and all her other Laotian students. Indeed it was a wonderful revelation for Jane, not least because she had discovered, from Cham's forty-five-minute nonstop talk, that he could speak English well enough to express his ideas.

In the face of Jane's delight I felt remorseful that I had missed this special day. When Cham came to the ESL room, I told him how sorry I was to have missed his stories. Cham gave me a big smile and said, "I can tell you again." He took out all his drawings, and began telling me about the temple. He told me what the temple looked like inside, how often people went to it, and what they did there. Then he described how his family's house was built and why it had to be built that way and how the families, relatives, and neighbors helped each other in the rice field during the harvest season. He recalled his school days—"The best part was playing soccer in the school field after the school." He gave the most details about life in the refugee camp: how they received their food ration and cooked their food; how he ran the risk of being put in jail for sneaking out from the wired fence to catch fish in the lake for his family; how they were punished by the police; how many sick people waited outside the camp clinic every day. . . .

He talked and talked without stopping for the whole class period, and I listened, as Jane and the others did, and said nothing. During this time, I would sometimes laugh with him, sometimes be silent when he recalled a bad experience, and sometimes try hard to hold back my tears. I was totally spellbound, immersed in Cham's stories, living through his past experience with him. Afterwards I asked him, "Are you going to write out all of these?" "Of course!" he replied. "That is what I *am* going to do next."

Through his drawings, Cham was able to organize his past memories and understand his past experience. He also communicated clearly with us. In her study of children's drawing, Ruth Hubbard (1989) concludes:

> Drawing is not just for children who can't yet write fluently, and creating pictures is not just part of rehearsal for real writing. Images at any age are part of the serious business of making meaning—partners with words for communicating our inner designs. (p. 157)

During the last few weeks of the school year, Cham worked on this project despite final exams and his other schoolwork. He drafted five stories. His English teacher helped him clarify his ideas, and Jane helped him edit his writing, polish the language, and type the stories. Within three weeks of the end of the school year, Cham had finished! His five stories—"The Buddhist Temple," "Houses in Laos," "Schools in Laos," "The Mekong River," and "Refugee Camps"—were a crowning achievement. Three of Cham's five stories appear below.

SCHOOLS IN LAOS

This is a picture of my school in Laos. The schools in Laos are small. Every city has only one school and most of the people go to it. In school we learn Lao and French.

School in Laos started at 8:00 am and goes to 12:30 pm every day. In Lao schools, most of the students wear uniforms. The boys wear short pants and white shirts. The girls wear skirts and white shirts.

If the students don't follow the school rules, they will be punished. They will have to stand on one foot for one half hour. They are also punished by having to clean the outside of the school. Most of the time the punishment is having to stand on one foot while holding a stick in your mouth. The teacher can hit the students.

In Laos, we don't have lunch in school, like in American schools. Sometimes the students bring their own food to eat during the school break. If you don't want to bring food to school, you can buy food outside of the school.

In school in Laos, many of the students are hurt by the teachers. Laos had no laws to protect children, like in America.

THE MEKONG RIVER

This is the picture of the Mekong River. It separates Laos and Thailand. The Mekong is about one mile wide. Most of the people in Laos use this river to transport food and other things. The Mekong is very deep, and has a lot of fish.

In 1972, the Communists took over the country. Many Lao people don't like the Communists because they tell the people what they should do. The people have to give their rice to the government. Many people try to escape from their own homeland because of the Communists.

Many people escape by boat, across the Mekong River to Thailand. Some people don't have money or a boat to escape. Some people try to make a raft to escape on.

Many people die in the Mekong because the weather is bad and the boats tip over in the rough waters. It's hard to escape from Laos because all around the river there are many soldiers. If the soldiers see you crossing the river, they will shoot you.

REFUGEE CAMPS

This is a picture of a refugee camp in Thailand. It is called the Napho Camp.

There are many buildings inside the camp. Every building there has ten rooms. There is one room for each family to live in. The rooms are very small. There are three thousand people in this camp.

The United Nations helps to give food to the refugees in the camp. Many people die in the camp because they don't get enough food and medicine. Water comes from a well. The U.N. gives meat, rice, vegetables, cooking oil and wood.

Life in the camp is hard. To get enough food, the people

have to sneak out of the camp. If the soldiers catch you, they will send you to jail for one month. There are many people in the camp who steal things from other people. There are many fires in the camp. If you burn your building, you will go to jail.

Most of the men and women work in the camp. They clean the camp. The children go to school. Most of the people stay in the camp from one year to ten years.

In the last week of the school year, Cham turned in his eight drawings and five stories. He chased after me when I was on my way to make copies of his work, telling me, "Would you please give them back to me as I will continue to work on them during the summer." Compared with Paw's attitude toward her "splendid paper" (as described in Chapter 4), Cham treasured his project.

Cham received a long response from his English teacher, the longest one he had ever received for an evaluation. It reads like this:

> Cham,
> Congratulations on this achievement! The ideas, the concerns, and the *work* that went into this project are to be commended.
> I truly enjoyed both the art and the written work. Combined, they give a good look at Laos and the differences between Laos and the U.S.A.
> I especially liked the part about the school. Here, you *show* many significant differences—they are many and profound.
> Finally, I hope you don't stop here. I know you have more to tell/write, and I hope you will do so!
> Oh—a grade? A   In both content and in work, you've put a lot into this project—Here is your reward.

At the high-school assembly held on the last day of school, Cham was given an award for the best achievement in the field of ESL study. Cham had realized his wildest dream, one he would never have believed a few months before, when he had said wistfully, "I wish I could improve my English and got an award for ESL. But I know that is hard. Dreams are hard to come true."

In this chapter, we have seen two different Chams: one who was sinking into the chasm of failure early in the year, and later one who, in the springtime of the year, flowered to become a writer, an artist, and a storyteller. The new freedom Cham found in the spring of the year released him to soar as an eagle, enabling him to give full play to his strengths and live up to his potential as a learner.

Cham's interest in his series of drawings and stories gave him the impetus to emerge during the last seven weeks at school as a person with integrity, with something to teach and tell. His metamorphosis demonstrates that our students need to learn to speak and write with their authentic voice as well as with the basic skills of literacy. Cham was finally able to express what he knew, what he felt, and what he wanted to tell. Most important, the discovery that Cham was able to write and had a voice in his writing was exhilarating for all.

 *Chapter Six*

Sy

Sy was the youngest of the nine children in the family. Each time when I visited his home, he either hid himself in his room or sat in the corner by himself. He never joined the conversation I carried on with his siblings or his parents. At school, it was even harder to talk to him.

Sy did not like to sit and chat with anybody, especially adults. I tried several times to talk with him, but every time I made him nervous. The more I tried, the more he avoided me. As I became a frequent visitor to his house, the other family members would talk to me like an old friend, but not Sy. I had a couple of formal interviews with him, and each time I tried to sound casual. By the end of the interview, he had become quite relaxed and started to say more and joke a little bit. By the next day, however, he would become the same shy and quiet Sy again. Our relationship never seemed to improve.

Since I could not have much personal contact with him, I sat in his English class and observed how he behaved in the classroom and among his peers. It was almost the same pattern as I found in him at home: Sy was unheard and invisible. Each time I visited him in English class or in the ESL room, I would make copies of something from his folder. He did not question me about what I was doing, as Tran did so frequently. When I asked him to talk about some of his work, Sy usually replied with "I don't know," "I forgot," or simply shrugged his shoulders. When he would not reply with one of these nonresponses, he would give me as short an answer as possible: "It's fun" or "I like it" or "I don't understand it."

I heard some other Laotian students complain that some boys at the school gave Sy a hard time by picking on him, but nobody heard any complaints from Sy himself. When I asked him about this, he did not say anything, but simply shrugged his shoulders and looked at the ground. Being unable to get Sy to express himself, I always had a feeling that I did not know him that well.

Sy had one year of school in Laos, but that was in a year when he was trying to escape from the country. Six of his brothers and sisters, two at a time, had left the country before him. A year later, with Tran, Sy also escaped to the Thai refugee camp. He grew up in the years when the family lived with uncertainty, worry, and fear. Before he was born, his father was taken away to a reeducation camp, and his six older brothers and sisters were sent to live with relatives. At the age of ten, Sy lived with his older brothers and sisters for the first time in the Thai refugee camp. He did not live with his father until the family came to America when Sy was eleven.

Sy could not remember anything about the Lao school he went to; as he told me, "I only had one year of school in Laos, and I even didn't remember how many days I went to the school. I didn't remember anything about the school." Sy recalled that in the refugee camp there was a school where the children could learn English every morning, but he could not remember anything he learned there. He said that his brothers and sisters all went to the Sunday school in the camp, where they became Christians, but he did not go. Paw told me that the family always thought Sy was young and immature, and nobody was serious about him: "He didn't like to sit in any class, that was okay for him. He just played all the time with other small kids. So he didn't learn anything."

Because Sy had little formal school experience before he came to America and understood no English when he started school in this country, his first school in Massachusetts had difficulties placing him. According to his age, he should be in sixth grade. Jane, the ESL teacher, told me:

Sy

When Sy first came to us, he didn't understand anything. No matter what we asked him, he would look at the other Laotian kids to let them translate for him. We just couldn't talk to him directly at all. I was told that when he was in school in Massachusetts, he was first put in the second grade. That must have been awful for him, as he was among tiny small kids. Then he was moved to the sixth grade, stayed there for a couple of months, then was moved down to the fourth grade. Before he first came to us, he was in a third-grade class. Last year, when he came to our school, we put him in a sixth-grade class.

Thus, in his first year of school in America, Sy was shifted to four different grades (second, sixth, fourth, and third). When I asked him about his first year in school, he told me, "I didn't understand anything. I didn't know anything the people said around me." In his first year in the Riverside school, he stayed in the sixth grade.

Sy spent most of his time that first year in the ESL room. He told me that he learned to speak English, to pronounce words, and to read textbooks that year. He could not remember any books or stories he read besides the ESL textbooks, nor had he written anything other than worksheets for his language exercises.

At the beginning of the seventh grade, I interviewed his English teacher, Susan. She could not tell me much about Sy as a student. When she talked about her six other Laotian students, she could tell me specifically about where each one was academically. Pointing to each of their names on the list, Susan would say things like, "She is an advanced student, she can go to Yale. . . . He is good, a college-bound kid. . . . That one is average, he has to work hard. . . . That girl is above average. She could be better if she put more effort into her work. . . ." But when she talked about Sy, she struggled for words:

I really don't know him. I don't know what his level is, or will be. I can't tell about him at this point at all. Neither did his former teachers when they gave him to me. They just couldn't say where he was. I need time to see, to know him.

170

Sy seldom read or wrote anything besides his schoolwork. When I asked what kind of reading or writing he enjoyed doing at home, he told me without hesitation, "I only read and write for the schoolwork, because I don't have any time to do anything else."

"How about some novels, newspapers, or even catalogues?" I pushed him to say more.

"No," Sy shook his head and said with eyes cast down, "I don't like to read. I like to play, play games. That's more fun than read and write. Yeah, sometimes I read funnies. They are like the cartoons I saw on TV, they are funny." He had a big smile on his face when he said that.

"How about writing?" I asked him.

"No, I hate to write. Yeah, I do write notes when I have to, to get permissions from the teacher to go to the library or some places at school."

Tran said that he rarely saw Sy doing schoolwork at home: "When he got home, he would sleep for a couple of hours, get up around 5:00 P.M. and then watch TV and play games." Sy's ESL teacher, Andy, told me a story about Sy:

> For a while Sy was so much into Nintendo. He played it all the time but never did his homework. I talked to him about it. That didn't work. I didn't know what I should do, as I knew if I told his father, he would be in big trouble, get beaten, something like that. So I didn't want that [to] happen to him. Finally I told his brothers. Then, when they saw him play Nintendo games again, they practically dragged him out of the room and forced him to do his homework.

This year, in the seventh grade, Sy was mainstreamed for every subject he took except for the one period a day in the ESL room. He enjoyed science and social studies the most. He said, "In science, you learn a lot of things, and in social studies, you can learn about different countries." He claimed that he learned the most in the home economics class: "I learned how to cook, how to sew, and do things. That was the most useful course I took." He disliked most his study-skills

171

class: "That is the most boring course I ever took." To him, the most difficult work was reading and writing: "I know it is the problems with my English. I wish that I could learn more English than reading and writing. I mean speaking English, the conversation English, not reading and writing. I need a lot of help with my English."

Like Tran, Paw, and Cham, Sy also knew that learning English was very important for him. Furthermore, he expressed several times his desire to become an ESL teacher: "I want to be an ESL teacher, to teach English to the children in the refugee camps in Thailand. But of course if I can make my English good." I was surprised to hear this. Sy was the one in his family who had the least memory of past schooling, including the English taught in the refugee camp. He had appeared to be the least interested of the four siblings in learning to read and write. However, he was the only one of the four to express a wish to become an ESL teacher and teach the refugee children in the camps. Tran wanted to be a businessperson, Cham a mechanic, and Paw a nurse. Becoming a teacher was the last thing these three would choose to do for a living. But in a letter to Andy, Sy wrote:

> Some day I would like to go back to Laos. My teacher Mr. Andy, he tells me thing in Laos are getting better.
>
> My school is too small there are too many people.
>
> My ESL teacher is very great and help me a lot. Sometimes I got very frustrated, but I want got better.
>
> I want good English when I go Laos so I can work for the Government. I would start school for the poor peoples.

Sy's seventh grade did not use the ranking system that was in place in the high-school grades. In his English class, Sy had more time and more freedom to read and write, and he spent less time on worksheets and tests. Of the work I collected from Sy for English, in one year, he had completed:

- twelve pages of reading journals
- two pieces on myth
- six pieces of free writing

- eighteen pieces of journal writing
- one set of worksheets on Latin roots
- one test on Latin roots
- one final exam.

Over ninety percent of the work I collected were actual writing samples—reading journals, creative writing, and daily journals—a sharp contrast to the work samples I had from Cham and Paw in their eleventh-grade B level English class.

The following sections describe Sy's experience of learning to write three different genres: reading-discussion writing, creative writing, and journal writing.

Reading-Discussion Writing

Reading-discussion writing refers to the writing the students do as part of a book discussion. Susan, the seventh-grade English teacher, had designed the curriculum to include two six-week units, one in December and January and the other in March and April. They were referred to as two units on reading-discussion.

In the first unit, the students were allowed to read any books they wished. They had to keep a reading journal in which they would discuss the books they read. During the six-week period, the teacher would discuss the elements of fiction writing in general terms every day in the class. Her class discussion covered such things as language, setting, plot, climax, and so forth. The homework assignment usually was to use the books they were reading as a reference to discuss what the teacher talked about that day. For instance, if the teacher talked about setting that day, the students' homework assignment was to discuss, in the reading journal, the setting of the books they were reading at the present.

The second unit focused on myths. During the six weeks of this unit, the teacher talked about the concept, genre, purpose, and sources of mythology. Meanwhile, the students were reading myths. They could choose to read whatever myths they liked. In the reading journal they then connected what

173

the teacher talked about in the class to the books they were reading.

Sy had the most difficulty with this type of writing. In the first two weeks of unit one, Sy read five short stories, but he did not do much writing in his journal. When I asked him if he liked the stories he read, he shrugged his shoulders and said, "Yeah, I think so. I chose them because they were short. I thought short stories were easy to read." I asked whether he understood the stories. He nodded his head and said, "Most of them. But I don't know how to do the homework." Susan said to me:

> I don't know what I am going to do with him. The only time he did his assignment was when I worked with him sentence by sentence. I can't work with him like that every time. When I asked him if he understood the direction, he nodded his head but he didn't do the homework. I just had to give him zero. What other choice is there?

In December, Sy received three zeroes for not doing the homework.

In the second unit, on mythology, Sy repeated the same pattern. He read a few myths, but he did not know how to discuss them. For instance, on the day Susan discussed the purposes of myth with the class, her homework assignment was: "What do you think is the most important purpose of your stories you read? (Use details to explain the purpose. You may think of one not covered in class today.)" Sy did not do his homework that night. The next morning he came to Andy (Sy's first period was in the ESL room with Andy) and said to him, "I have to write an essay, but I don't know what it is." Without knowing the assignment, Andy could not help him. That day Sy went to the class without having done his homework. During the six weeks of mythology discussion, Sy did the homework only twice. Susan became frustrated with him again and told me in April:

> I don't know why, but I don't see that Sy has made much progress in my class this year. Sometimes I feel I should take some ESL courses myself to understand students like Sy. I give

homework every day, but he seldom does it. Maybe he is too exhausted after a whole day's work at the school. Maybe I should give him something more solid and concrete to do, like sentence combining, or another set of homework exercises. I don't know what I should do with him right now.

In order to understand Sy better, I observed him in English class for a week and interviewed him during the time the class was studying mythology. He appeared very attentive in the class. He sat at the front by himself. He jotted down whatever the teacher wrote on the blackboard, but he did not write down what the teacher or the students talked about. Many students interacted with the teacher, but Sy rarely made any comments or even showed any response with his body language. After the class, I asked him how much he understood of what the teacher and the other students said. He told me, "A little, not much." I asked, "Is that the reason that you couldn't do your homework?" He nodded his head and said to me with his head down and in a low, guilty-sounding voice, "I couldn't understand much in the class and didn't know what the teacher wanted us to write." Mike Rose (1989) described the alienation that students like Sy often suffer in the classroom:

> People are taking notes and you are taking notes. You are taking notes on a lecture you don't understand. You get a phrase, a sentence, then the next loses you. It's as though you're hearing a conversation in a crowd or from another room—out of phase, muted. (p. 168)

This must be what Sy felt but could not express.

Of the few homework assignments Sy did in the reading-discussion period, one was a summary of a story he had read:

THE KING OF THE CROCODILES

One day has one family live in their farm with a beautiful daughter. One morning he went out to farm at his field. When he get there, he saw a crocodile lying on the wheat, he wicked mad at him. He start to throw the stones at him. Then he went home. and the next day he came again and he did again. That time the big crocodiles came up and try to bit him and hurt him but he saving his own life to kill. Then they said to the father bring your daughter to marry our king. The father wanted to see his daughter under the water. He went to his field look for crocodile about he want to visit his daughter. The crocodile tell him to "deep into the water until you found a castle." he did what they said. After he visit them he became rich, because the king of the crocodiles give him a land, diamonds and something else.

This was a passable summary of the story. Susan told me that Sy rarely had problems writing a summary if he understood the story.

The other homework Sy did in this period was in answer to the question "How did the Greek myths get into English?" When I asked him how he was able to complete this assignment, Sy told me, "That might be the only thing I understood of what the teacher said, and I took good notes, too." To answer the question "How did the Greek myths get into English?" Sy wrote:

A person came from Greek with a story in their mind. he told stories to persons who know how to write in English. Then they wrote the story in a book.

This answer repeated his class notes almost verbatim. It reminded me of what the social studies teacher said of Sy:

He is a fact person. He can remember facts very well, and always gets good grades on fact sheets. But he is not creative and imaginative. When he answers questions, he can only tell you the surface meaning, but can't go further in the discussion. That is why he can't write good essays.

Sy's answer to the question about Greek myths was consistent with what the social studies teacher said about him. He repeated the teacher's words to answer the question and did not show any understanding of the text.

Looking through Sy's twelve pages of reading-journal entries, I found that there was an obvious gap between Sy's work and the teacher's expectations for reading discussion. He tried to answer the questions the teacher had asked, but what he wrote did not really meet the requirements.

For example, Sy read the book *Hatchet*. One set of the questions the teacher raised was:

> Do you like the book? Do you think Brian will survive? Will he be rescued? What if he isn't found? Write answers to these questions before you read more.

Sy answered these questions only in part:

> Yes, he is because he have the place to live and has food to eat.

It seemed that Sy only saw certain parts of the teacher's questions as necessary to answer. The following dialogue I had with Sy explains Sy's thinking.

> Danling: Why didn't you answer all the teacher's questions?
> Sy: I did.
> Danling: You didn't say you liked the book or not.
> Sy: I don't have to.
> Danling: Why?
> Sy: I won't read it if I don't like it.
> Danling: You didn't answer "Will he be rescued?" or "What if he isn't found?"
> Sy: Of course he will be rescued. You don't have to say it, otherwise how did people know the story. He will be found, for sure, he will.
> Danling: You don't think "what if" would happen?
> Sy: No.

From this conversation, I could see that Sy saw no need to answer questions that were self-evident or had answers that were implied. In his mind, there was no need to answer questions just for the sake of answering questions. I remembered Tran's similar sentiments when we had discussed his book report. He was unwilling to follow the step-by-step way to arrive at an answer when it was either evident or implied, and Sy felt the same way when he encountered his teacher's questions.

Shirley Brice Heath (1983) defined this gap between learning and teaching as a cultural gap between real life and school life. In *Ways with Words*, she showed that black children had difficulty answering the teacher's questions when they were presented in a style that was unfamiliar to them. Many of the teacher's questions were intended just for language instruction, not a real inquiring. The black children struggled to answer the questions not because they did not know the answers, but because they did not know why the teacher asked questions to which she already knew the answer. Sy and Tran's experience was similar to that of the black children's in Heath's study.

Once the teacher asked Sy to evaluate his own writing, what he did revealed a similar cultural gap. To her assignment

> Skim through your journal. Which is your best entry? Identify it and explain why it is the best.

Sy wrote:

> I think he feel very happy and have more safe now from porcupine and other different insects like mosquitos.
> Now Brian has the place to live and he not very hungry again.

The teacher had asked Sy to discuss his own writing, but it did not occur to him that that was what the teacher wanted: "I thought the teacher asked me to talk about the best part of the story, not my writing. I don't know how to talk about my writing. It is the teacher's job." Self-evaluation was strange to him. From his written answer, I had thought he had simply misinterpreted the teacher's question. What he said reveals that even if he understood what the teacher wanted from him, he could not do it because he believed that evaluation was the teacher's job, not his. Sy's hesitation in evaluating his own work was understandable. Being programmed in the school system—and at home—to be mainly a recipient, not an instigator of evaluation, he had never had a chance to evaluate himself.

In the discussion assignments, most of the teacher's questions were geared toward the elements of fiction writing: the language the author used, the setting, the plot, or the climax. Sy had a lot of problems with this kind of assignment because he often did not understand the meaning of the term, and he did not always know how to discuss a certain aspect of writing. Here is an example of Sy's discussion of the setting:

Question: How do you know what the setting is?

Sy's answer: The setting in my story is in the middle of the wood.

Question: Summarize ideas about how important the setting is to the plot.

Sy's answer: In some stories the setting is important to the plot. For example the story about boy who live in the middle of the wood, had to be happening in the wood.

Some stories the setting does not important to the plot. A example the stories can not be happening in the middle of the city.

In the first question, the teacher expected Sy to discuss the language the author used to create the setting, but Sy only answered where the story took place. In the second question, the teacher wanted Sy to discuss the relationship between the setting and the plot, and Sy offered little more than he had in his first response. Obviously he knew what a setting was, but he did not know how to discuss it. More examples revealed that he did not fully grasp what was questioned:

1. Find and copy the climax of the story, explaining why that event is the climax.

Sy's answer:
[Sy copied page 157 as the climax.]
But there is difference not, he thought—there really is a difference. I might be hit but I'm not done. When the light comes I'll start to rebuild. I still have the hatchet and that's all I had in the first place.
When the airplane crashed in the middle of the forest on above the water of the lake and when he survived or living alone in the forest.

Because the pilot who drive the airplane got heart attack that why he live alone in the middle of forest.

He very tough boy and he never give up to survive in the middle of the forest.

2. How is the information organized?

Sy's answer:

The Hatchet stories, the best I has been reading Because it was about the boy survive in the middle of the forest. When the pilot got heart attack and the airplane crash on the lake then Brian swam out of the water but his leg it very hurt him then he found the cave and he made the arrow to hunt animals for food.

Instead of discussing climax and the organization of information, Sy talked about the main ideas of the story and the main character. When he was asked to discuss "what you like the least about the book," he misunderstood "least" to mean "most" and answered accordingly:

I like the book it was about a boy, he is his name is Brian Robeson, he went to see his father in north Canada but airplane got crash in the middle of the forest, he very confusion because he doesn't know which way he gonna going.

When he was asked to write a book review, he wrote a similar response:

The Hatchet stories the best book I has been reading, it was about the boy survive in the middle of the forest.

Brian personalities is was very smart and confusion. he smart when he dive in the water and find something in the plane, confusion when he don't know where he were.

He very tough boy, when the moose try to kill but the moose can't. Then the wind destroy Brian shelter, but he never give up.

To the four directives (find and explain the climax, write about how the information is organized, describe the part he liked the least, and write a book review), Sy summarized the main idea and wrote about the main character each time. This was, in his own words, "what I learned about the story." He could comprehend the story he read, but he did not know how to analyze it.

I observed how Sy read *Hatchet* with Andy in the ESL room. He and Andy took turns reading, paragraph by paragraph. Sometimes Andy would ask Sy to tell him what the paragraph meant, and sometimes he would just let Sy go on with his reading. If Sy had no idea of what he read, Andy would explain it to him. With Andy's help, Sy read one paragraph after another. It took them about three weeks (from January 10 to February 1) to finish reading the one-hundred-and-ninety-five-page book.

Sy's cultural and linguistic barriers and his scant early schooling contributed to Sy's present difficulty understanding the teacher in class and following the teacher's directives for the reading discussion. *Hatchet* was one of the few books Sy had ever read. It took a lot of effort for him to understand the story. After each chapter, Sy could only manage to describe the events of the story; he was unable to interpret the text, and he did not understand the formal elements of fiction. Hence, he was confused and unable to analyze the story. His limited knowledge of English and his limited early reading experience precluded analytical reading for Sy. With only two years of formal schooling, he was not equipped to talk about setting, plot, and climax. These terms were foreign to him even in his native language.

The new language, the new concepts, and the new non-textbook genre overwhelmed Sy. His introduction to reading-discussion writing was like moving away from "the personalized, contextualized, orally expressed knowledge of home to the depersonalized, decontextualized, primarily written knowledge of the classroom" (Goleman 1986, p. 136). In his school experience, Sy daily tried to make sense of strange concepts in a new language and in a new context. No wonder he had to go to bed every afternoon as soon as he got home. There was too much translation—linguistic, cultural, and conceptual—for him to do every day at school.

Free Writing

Sy's English class had a free-writing period, when the students could write about anything they wanted. They would choose their own topics and write at their own pace. Susan, the teacher, scheduled this activity twice a year for her students: once early in the year (from October to November), and again toward the end of the year (from the second half of April to early June).

Free writing was a new concept to Sy. At first he did not know how to do it, so he would work on writing assignments from his other courses, such as social studies and science. Sy did this for a couple of weeks. Later, he wrote a piece about his life in the Thai refugee camp. It was a short piece, but it was something he knew about.

CAMP IN THAILAND

In the camp the government gave us food every Monday, Wednesday and Friday like fish, meat, vegetable. Every group have the leader run get something the government gave to us. and every Friday they gave to us the rice. One person get 4.5 pound in the camp every house has they own kitchen.

Every day we went to school, after that me and friends we went to swimming play turns or sometimes we go fishing.

When the teacher asked the class to "choose the best piece you wrote and talk about it (explain why you like it the best)," Sy wrote:

I talk about my family live in camp of Thailand, first we came we don't have any money. When we stay longer as sister found a good job. She work for government of camp Thailand. They pay one hundred bucks for a mother. Her boss is the American. I like "Camp in Thailand" this talk about myself and my family.

"Camp in Thailand" was the first piece Sy wrote that was freely expressed. He saw it as his best piece. He had no trouble making a choice and explaining why it was the best. He did not wait and let his teacher select one for him. When he was familiar with his topic, he had no problems talking about his writing and evaluating himself.

The second piece Sy wrote, shortly after Halloween, was called "Trick or Treting Day":

TRICK OR TRETING DAY

One scare dark night me and Flutty went to down street near the school. it is halloween Flutty and I were trick or treting, I wear the werewolf costume. When I going to the next house and knock the door. The old woman came out. When she saw me, her face turn to yellow and her body start to shaking because she think I'm the Real Werewolf. When I said "Trick or Treting" louger, she close the door she doesn't give me a candy. After I and Flutty was walk home but when we walk acrost in front of school heard the sound scream. It came from in side the school. Then I go close I saw two mans tie the girl on the chair. When I walk to the back of the school, the door is openning. Me and Flutty walk in to save the girl from the thief. Then we ran out of school. The thief saw me and short me on my leg than the police heard the sound of gun. Then they come and the thief run away. Now everything is very save.

The End.

This was the first piece of fiction Sy ever wrote. He said that he enjoyed writing this piece, and he did it almost entirely on his own. He told me that he did go trick or treating with a friend and showed me the mask he had bought for himself. But most of the details in his stories were his creations. He said that he got his ideas from what he saw on TV. He had written a fictional story by using his real experience in combination with what he saw on TV. Here Sy had revealed himself as someone who could create and imagine, in contrast to what his other schoolwork had led people to believe, that he was simply a "fact person" who could remember things but could not analyze or imagine.

Four months later, the class entered the second phase of free-writing activity. This time, Sy started out differently; he did not bring in assignments from other classes, as he had done before. By this time he seemed to be used to writing with free choice. He wanted to write a fairy tale. He knew what he wanted to say but had difficulties writing it. So he went to his sister, Paw, for help. He told her his ideas in Lao, mixed with

183

some English words that had no equivalent in Lao. The story that Paw translated from what Sy told her was like this:

> Once upon a time there was a small kingdom that had a king. He loved to go hunting for fun. One day he went to hunt [where] he [was] used to going. But today he saw a very beautiful deer that he never saw before. The king go after the deer until he founded a small hut. He found a very beautiful lady and a deer that he looking for in there.

After I read it, I asked Paw how she helped Sy, and she said:

> Sometimes Sy would get so frustrated as he couldn't say in Lao or English. His face turned so red, but he couldn't find words for his ideas. He waved his hands, tried to find words for it, but he couldn't express it. Then I would help him, say, "Do you mean this?" or "Do you mean that?" I also helped him with transitions. For instance, he didn't know how to start the story. I told him in fairy tale, you often started the story with "once upon a time." That's the same in Lao. Or use "then" something like that.
>
> It took us about an hour to do this story. He had all his ideas ready. I think he got his ideas from the cartoon he watched on TV. He loved to watch cartoons.

Sy added that his ideas for the fairy tale came "not just from TV, but also from the reading of myth stories." The class had just finished the unit on mythology, and Sy had read quite a few myths. This fairy tale had the flavor of a story Sy had summarized earlier.

I interviewed Susan about her views of Paw's translation for Sy. She told me:

> At first when I saw Sy copy the story in class, I thought he was cheating. When he told me that it was all his ideas and his sister only translated them for him, I thought that was all right. As long as it was his story, it should be okay at the beginning. I will see what will happen next.

As soon as Sy finished his first story, he had ideas for his second one. He went to Andy and said to him, "This time I want to write a story called 'Lazy Cat.'" Andy responded enthusiastically, "Great! Tell me about your crazy cat." With facial expressions and hand and body gestures, Sy told Andy his story. Andy said, "Oh, you mean a *lazy* cat. I thought you said a *crazy* cat. Okay, Let's start working on it."

Like Paw, Andy helped Sy with transitions, vocabulary, and grammar. However, Andy did not write the story for Sy but let him write down his own ideas. Every day they both worked on the story. A week later, Sy finished his story of Lazy Cat. It was the longest one he had ever written.

LAZY CAT

Lazy cat living in big city. he like sleep all day long. Sleeping is a favorite thing he like to do. Before he sleep, he eats a tone of food. Late at night he was out with another cat and get drink. Then he and his friends made lots of noise in the street.

One day his master, Linda, went to the kitchen to get something to eat. She saw a mouse run across the floor. she jump up on a chair and screamed louder, but not loud enough to wake lazy cat.

Linda pick up the broom ran to the lazy cat and hit him because to wake him to catching a mouse. Lazy cat yawned slowly open his eyes and meowed then went back sleep again. She hit him harder this time. Lazy cat wake up very fast and jump on Linda and he scratched her and Linda grap the cat and throw him out of window.

Linda said "you stupid cat stay out until you catch a mouse!"

What Linda didn't know it that lazy cat was very afraid of the mouse this is why he sleeps all day and got drunk at night. After he kick out the house, he was disappear until 37 days after. He went back home to the town but he got accident and he die by the car.

The End

I asked Andy about the differences in helping Sy with his own story versus helping him in the reading-discussion format. Andy said:

It was easy to help him with his creative-story writing, because he had all the ideas, I only helped him with the language. He got stuck mostly with the unknown words, not ideas. He knew what he wanted to say. Sometimes I helped him with grammar when it got too messy, but I didn't correct every sentence he wrote. I didn't want to stop him all the time. It was hard to help him write when he didn't have any ideas. That happened when he had to write an essay, or something to discuss the books he read. He not only didn't know what to write, but didn't understand the requirement. Sometimes he would come to me and say, "I have to write an essay, but I don't know what it is." How can I help him when he doesn't even know the assignment? I can't help him when that happens.

Sy turned in little homework during the reading-discussion writing sessions, but he turned in all the homework for the free-writing ones. His behavior was noticeably different during these two writing times. From being markedly quiet in the class or ESL room during reading-discussion writing, he became quite animated with Andy and with his classmates in their small writing group during the free-writing periods. After Sy wrote "Lazy Cat," Susan also noticed Sy was beginning to emerge from his shell. She told me, "Sy has become very friendly to me recently. Whenever he sees me, he speaks to me loudly and clearly, and with a big smile on his face, 'Hi, Mrs. M. How are you doing today?' I feel really good about it." Perhaps because Sy had "joined the literacy club" (Smith 1988), he felt better about himself.

It did not take Sy long to figure out what he wanted to write after "Lazy Cat." "I want to write a story like Robin Hood," he told Andy in the ESL room. "It is adventure, has a hero, who helps poor people and fight the rich. That is the kind of story I like most. I love to watch those kinds of movies." This third story, his last for the second free-writing session, was called "Simple Robin Hood."

Susan was very excited to see Sy's progress as a writer. One day in June, a few days before the final exams, she told me:

> Sy has made a lot of progress in this period. I didn't see him get frustrated. He never missed any writing assignments. I saw him more active in his group. He asked about the words he

didn't know. Once I saw him ask Tim "how to write the word *cuble* . . . , *cuble*, it means *two, two*." Finally Tim understood that he meant *couple*. One day I observed him revise and edit his writing while he was copying it. I saw him shift certain sentences, change the words, underline the names, and capitalize the words he hadn't done in the draft. I am so excited to see what he was doing. He has indeed made a lot of progress. I almost gave up on him a couple of months ago.

Sy had made progress and had shown he knew how to write fiction. In the final exam, Susan asked the class to evaluate their own writing for the year:

> Compare two of your better pieces of writing. How are they alike, how are they different? What makes each a good piece?

Sy wrote that he thought "Lazy Cat" and "Simple Robin Hood" were the best stories he wrote this year because:

> In the beginning of my two best pieces, I talking about where they living, what they like to do in the day, and In the middle of my stories I put what problems they have.
>
> This both stories are different when the place was happening and personal.
>
> The idea that come from my brain are make the both stories are good pieces and I also think the dictionary for helping me all this year.

In the first paragraph, he mentions the setting (where they are living), the characters (what they like to do during the day), the plot, and conflict (what problems they have). Though he did not use those terms to describe his stories, his evaluation showed that he knew that stories needed those elements to make them whole, and he had included them.

The best part of his self-evaluation, I think, was the last paragraph. It declares his understanding of what made his writing good ("The idea that come from my brain are make the both stories are good pieces") and his realization of the importance of using reference books in writing ("I also think the dictionary for helping me all this year"). Five months previously, Sy had refused to evaluate his writing, as he thought that was only the teacher's job. By year's end, he had learned how to write self-expressively, how to use a reference book to find the right words, and how to evaluate his work.

Journal Writing

Toward the end of the school year, Susan asked her students to keep a journal at home, writing at least three entries each week. In the journal, they could jot down personal observations, private thoughts, comments about their reading and writing, or anything else. As Susan said:

> I want them to become sensitive to their surroundings and learn to describe their observations and thoughts. I think journal writing will help them develop sensitivity, imagination, thinking and also their writing skills.

This proved to be the easiest genre of all for Sy. He did not seek much help from teachers or from his sister, as he had done on other occasions. During the six weeks of journal writing, Sy wrote eighteen entries. Each one revealed something about Sy that I had never seen before. I had perceived him as extremely quiet, passive and obedient at home and in school. But in his journals, I discovered new dimensions to Sy. First, I found that he was a storyteller and loved to tell his stories. I had found earlier, in the free-writing sessions, that he could tell good stories, but now, in the pages of his personal journal, he expressed himself even more freely. In one of the pieces he describes his dream.

> One day I went to some where but no direction to show where I'm going. I keep looking to. From my house to the place I never see before, I told myself where am I. But later I heard a sound of my mom talk to me but I don't know where the sound come from. Later the sound was disappeared. I keep think in my mind what I got to do to get out of the here. Later I said to my mind "I get the better idea to get out of the here." I heard the noise again this time. The noise is so louder, my ear can't stand until I run fast I can to beginning where I starting, But the noise still following me. After that I sit down on

road side to breathe because my legs is so tired and my heart is start shake harder. Now I walking on road side slow when I look down saw nothing but the tree couple minutes ago I didn't see the tree. That very Amazing thing happening to me. I said to myself bite yourself. After I did is not harm my skin. I say to my mine "I know it is the dream" when I wake up in the real world I ran downstairs and open the door that was my big brother was knock the door.

In many entries, he simply talked about what he did, felt, or thought each day. The thing that struck me most was that he did not record "bed to bed" stories, like many inexperienced journal writers tend to do, but focused on one incident in the day. Here are some examples.

Yesterday me and my friends ride a bike through downtown to got our pizza that we order. he promise me if I let him borrow my money he let me used the video game for two days, but he lie to me. I got mad at him and kick his bike on the back wheel of his bike is almost broke.

Today I don't know what happening in my mind. Everything turn me borry and made me sick of it.

I hope some my cousin come over visit my house this weekend and or my father lets us go to the theater to watching the movies call "Don't tell mom the babysit is dead." This movie wick funny and interesting movie that the way I saw in the commercial after the movie I watching in the TV.

Today I ride my brother bike to school to watching the baseball game. Our school won the game by scores 13 to 4. After the game I went to Woodland Drive to play basketball with my friend. This time on basketball game I'm not very careful but I try to lay up lot I fell down on floor I used my had to protect my body but went I hit the gournd I used only my right hand and my right hand I got hurd until now.

Today I talk to my mom about this summer, where we gonna go and who we gonna go visit, she tell me we going to visit your father's friend in Tennesse after that we going to New York city to visit my cousin and we going to ride a ship to the Status of Liberty.

Sy

These four short pieces are like four snapshots of Sy's life outside of school. They are simple and very focused and clear. They show glimpses of Sy's personality, his moods and feelings, his interests and activities, and some of his family life. Certainly the first entry shows a fiery side of Sy, one I had not seen in him before. Each piece has the potential for further story development.

In some of his journal entries, Sy reveals himself as an observer of nature, and as someone who reflects on his observations.

> On this weekend me and my friends riding a bike around Riverside. I saw many things. the first beautiful thing I saw in the tree on the countryside. Animals ran across the road, some of them they play up on the tree. A people start to farm and growing some fruit and vegetable. We saw a man who own the horses farm practice horse ride.
>
> I think if I ride them I might got kick by the horse. The horse is the one big animal. The horse is the one animal danger if you don't know how to control them.

> This morning I got almst missing the bus because I wake up too late.
>
> During I was in the bus I look up into the sky, the color is blue and white, the sound of bird up in the tree and old man spend his time on fishing.

He describes the animals, trees, birds, sky, and people he observes like one learning to sketch the scenery around him. The entries were simple and interesting. Sy did them without worrying about the length or the structure of the writing. I agreed with Susan that this was a good way to encourage students to write about their surroundings in a sensitive way. I could see that Sy's pieces had potential as poems.

Most surprising for me were Sy's entries about his wishes. They exposed his imagination and thoughtful introspection, which were seldom apparent in his other work, and also uncovered a deeper side that I had not seen before.

If I had a magic lamp I want to be the rich boy in the world and a good life, buy a house and has my own business.

I think if I flying like the birds, first fly in Europe to Paris, I hear many peoples said "In there they have many thing it very beautiful" I hope someday I will go France and have some hot tea.

I wish I could fly like a bird to travel to every country I want, but I got a problem about how I gonna to change form like a bird and it change to a bird how I gonna fly over the ocean. The ocean is so far flying across it. Many people or the big animals thought me to a food and they gonna hunt me down from sky to the ground then how I gonna to escape from them.

Sy seems to be using the symbol of the bird to represent freedom. Sy and his family left their home country and came to America to be free. They were like birds themselves. His journals were where Sy, flying like a bird, could freely express his wishes and his desires through his imagination, where he could relax and not worry, where rules, deadlines, and special forms were not binding him.

Reading through his journal, I discovered many dimensions to Sy: he was a typical teenager with a strong personality, a boy who liked to dream, a young man full of imagination, a thinker, a reader, and a storyteller. Sy's journal was the vehicle for his self-expression and his self-discovery, the place where he had found his authentic voice.

In this chapter, we have seen three different Sys emerge as he learned to write in different genres. In the reading-discussion writing phase, Sy was a lost and confused learner, so much so that he did not even know how to seek help from his teachers and peers. He rarely turned in his homework assignments, and his writing did not meet the teacher's expectations. The teacher, herself confused by Sy's confusion, could only grade him according to his effort. She said, "I couldn't measure his writing with the same standard as I used for the others, so I graded him according to his efforts. If he did his work, I gave him points. If not, I gave zeroes." Sy got many zeroes in the reading-discussion writing phase of the English class.

When the time came for creative story writing, Sy could take command and make progress. He still needed help, but he knew how to seek help from his sister, from the ESL teacher, from his peers, and from the dictionary. He knew how to draw upon sources for his ideas: from his personal experience, from the TV shows he saw, and from his readings. In the free-writing phase, Sy grew as a writer through constant writing, talking, and reading.

Sy surfaced as a real flesh-and-blood person, flying free as a bird in his journal entries. He was self-reliant when writing in his daily journal, much more so than he had been in the earlier reading-discussion and free-writing phases. He sought resources from within his own brain (a word he used a lot), expressed himself from his own heart, and gave full freedom to his imagination and thinking. He freed himself by writing in his journal.

As we have seen, the reading-discussion format for writing was the most difficult for Sy. It demanded thorough understanding of the text being read and of the techniques employed in creating the text; it proved to be far too advanced an activity for Sy, who needed a lot of time to understand the text itself, and was not able at that stage of his language development to discuss the reading in the way the teacher expected. In that setting, Sy was on unfamiliar ground, with little connection to what he knew. That was why he appeared lost and passive, and simply parroted the facts in the reading-discussion writing.

Free writing allowed Sy to connect his own interests and experience with writing. He was more at ease with free writing than he was with the reading discussion, and in the free-writing format he began to talk about his past life and create stories through the combination of his personal experiences, the stories he had read, and his favorite TV shows. Through storytelling, Sy visited familiar and favorite make-believe people and things, much like having his own private

Disneyland with Lazy Cat, Robin Hood, and the deer in a hut. His language problems faded when he found ways to solve them, and Sy began to use language as a key to unlock his own ideas. Once he had the ideas, the tools were an arm's length away.

Sy's journals were his alter ego. They opened up parts of himself that even he had been unaware of, as Murray (1987) says about his writing: "I write to explore. I write to find out what I have lived, what I have felt, what I have thought. I use language as a tool of seeing and understanding" (p. 266). Through journals, Sy discovered his world and himself. Journal writing sharpened Sy's sense of his surroundings, and it became the key to his heart and mind, exposing his potential as a writer. In fact, Sy had the fewest language difficulties when he could speak from his own heart and experience. Sy's growing experience and development as a writer underscores what Graves (1985) claims: "All children can write" if we give them time and the freedom to write what they know and what they want to say.

Sy was lucky to have a teacher who provided him not only with instruction, but with time, opportunities, and freedom to learn to write—to explore, to struggle, to take risks, and to grow as a reader and writer. Compared with the experiences of his brothers and sister, and with his own past learning experiences, Sy had improved the most as a learner, considering how far behind he was at the beginning of the school year. He had been able to move a distance away from the problems that had surrounded him and had started to become a self-confident reader, thinker, and writer. He was "in gear" to continue on and on.

On the last day of the school year, Sy went to Susan and asked her in a very low voice with his head bent down, "Mrs M., what grade will I be next year?"

Susan answered, "The eighth grade."

"What? You mean I will go up to the eighth grade?" said Sy in a raised voice, as he lifted his head. He could not believe his ears!

"Yes." Susan in turn raised her voice and pronounced every word slowly and clearly. "Of course you will go up to the eighth grade!"

As soon as Susan finished her sentence, Sy jumped high and shouted, "Wow! I will *go up* to the eighth grade! I will *be* in the *eighth* grade! Thank you! Thank you, Mrs. M!" Sy turned around and, with a loud voice and flushed face, told everybody who happened to pass by, "I will go up to the eighth grade!"

Susan stood there, rolled her eyes good-naturedly, and said softly: "Why does he thank me? He earned it."

If Sy continues to progress as he did in the seventh grade, he will continue to "go up" the ladder of literacy in his new culture.

Conclusion

In this book, we hear the voices of Tran, Paw, Cham, and Sy. Through their voices, we may enter their minds and understand their feelings. The conversations they had with me brought me closer to them and gave them opportunities to open their minds to others and express their thoughts and feelings. However, we can hardly hear them when they are in classrooms, especially in low-level classes, where we see them silently sitting in corners, far away from others, impassively working on worksheets and tests. Their schoolwork does not encourage them to speak, share, and get to know others, but buries them in decontextualized words and meaningless language skills. They are too busy to speak and to use language for any real purpose other than grades. Ironically, the harder they work, the less they can speak, and the farther removed they become from others. Few people at school, including their teachers, know much about them, and they do not know anything about the people they are with every day.

The Importance of Talk

Britton (1972) greatly values talk, which he thinks is critical not only to adolescents' pursuit of ideas but to their establishing relationships with others. He asserts that talk is the most likely means by which students first investigate, explore, and organize new fields of interest, and connect with others. Students with limited English like Tran, Paw, Cham, and Sy need to talk in order to connect with others, to understand the people around them, and to explore the knowledge and the world they came to join. Each of them has expressed a burning desire: "I wish I could speak just like the others"; "I wish I could understand what is on their mind"; "I want to be just like them." But the schooling Tran, Paw, and Cham received has provided little opportunity for them to connect with others, nor has it invited them to be part of the community. For three years, immersed in the English language community, surrounded by Americans and working daily on their English, they still have great difficulty making themselves understood. Their heavy accent, their lack of English vocabulary, and their limited knowledge of the new culture mark their distance from others. They all know what they need in order to move closer to others, so they work hard at their English. But their hard work has helped them little to lessen their accent, enlarge their daily vocabulary, or gain knowledge of their new culture. We have seen how Cham and Paw spend most of their time learning vocabulary words from the spelling book, but the learning has not helped them increase their language proficiency for routine communication in the English-speaking world.

From Paw's different learning experiences in her A and B level English classes, we see there is a difference between high-level and low-level classes in the structure of learning. The higher-level class gives students more freedom of choice in reading and writing, more encouragement of analytical and creative thinking, and more opportunities for communication and sharing, in book talks, class discussions, debates, and writing responses. Goodlad (1984) found in a survey of 1,106 classrooms in thirty-eight schools that in the first through third grades, teaching involves a lot of interaction between teachers and children and among children, but that interaction and collaboration grow less and less frequent in the higher grades. In high schools, teaching tends to take the form of lecturing or seat work. Goodlad observed that "on the average, over seventy-five percent of class time was spent on instruction and nearly seventy percent of this was usually teacher to students" (1984, p. 229). Students tracked at low levels may be in a worse situation than Goodlad described, because they are considered to lack basic skills and concentration skills. Therefore, even more emphasis is placed on spelling words, completing pretest exercises, and working silently on individual worksheets and quizzes. They do not read and write as much as others in high-level classes, are required to do little critical thinking, and are rarely encouraged to talk and share their learning. Students like Tran, Paw, Cham, and Sy desperately need to know and connect with others through mutual sharing. They need to find out what is around them and see positive models of their new culture among their peers. But speaking is the language activity Tran, Paw, Cham, and Sy have done the least at school.

Britton (1972) sees talk as a necessary step to reading and writing: "Talk . . . prepares the environment into which what is taken from reading may be accommodated; and from that amalgam the writing proceeds" (p. 166). Vygotsky (1978) asserts that learning happens first through social interaction. Talk helps us make sense of what we read and helps external knowledge become our own. Conversation is an essential step in writing: it helps stimulate our thinking, organize our thoughts, and search for words in our ideas.

Individuality in Ethnicity

Many studies on the learning patterns of minority students (Ogbu 1974, 1978, 1983, 1987; Trueba 1987, 1988a, 1990b; Gibson 1987b; Caplan, Choy, and Whitmore 1991) have shown that quietness and withdrawal are typical of Asian students. Their silence is attributed to their ethnic culture. As an Asian myself, I do, to some extent, agree with these findings. Asian culture does stress listening more than speaking because being modest is considered an important virtue. The culture does not encourage youngsters to speak up in front of authorities, as respect and obedience are stressed for the younger generation. In student-centered and critical-thinking-oriented classrooms, the silence of these students can become a problem. No matter how successful Asian students may be, they are often considered too quiet, too passive, reserved, and unreachable. Successful students tend to be seen as too aloof and not contributing to the learning community, while low achievers are believed to be slow and unable to think.

Having been raised in Asian culture, I can discuss this issue from personal experience. I am quiet most of the time in a crowd or in a formal setting, but I am not passive or reserved. There are many reasons for me to keep quiet. As a newcomer, I am confronted with many unfamiliar things in the culture; I need to learn more about them through listening. Also, as a non-native English speaker, I need more time than others to phrase my thoughts before I speak, especially in a formal setting; as a result, often the topic changes before I get a turn. Then I am too polite to drag the attention of the crowd back to myself. As Tran said, "We don't do 'small talk' in public or in front of many people." In the Chinese culture we tell our children, "You shouldn't speak up if you are not a hundred percent sure of what you are going to say." So we are always careful of what we say, because we are very conscious of our image to others. We are also taught to control our emotions in public and among strangers. That is why we do not often see many Asian students burst out with anger and frustration in public: they are afraid of appearing silly or to be thought of as showing off or wasting the time of others. Conformity is valued more than uniqueness. I am talkative and sometimes very loud among friends. Often, when I get excited, I tend to interrupt others. (In the Chinese culture, we do not have to wait for others to finish speaking; we can just cut in. We do not consider this to be rude, but a sign of our engagement in the conversation.) I do enjoy talking, and I want to contribute, but many times it is not an easy thing for me to do, especially among people I do not know well or on a topic I am not a hundred percent sure of.

Because of my own experiences, I understand perfectly well why many Asian students are so quiet in their classrooms. In order to encourage them to speak up and participate in class activities, teachers have to build classrooms into friendly communities through constant group sharing and cooperative group activities. Studies have shown that Asian students do better and are more active in cooperative than in individual situations (Trueba 1990b; Gibson 1988). What and how teachers do and say things greatly affects the atmosphere of the class community. Teachers' sharing of their own stories is an important way to set an intimate tone for their classes and is a good model for a learning community of equal partners. I will never forget how I relaxed and was encouraged to speak out by my professors' sharing of their thoughts and stories. What they had to say not only aroused talk among the students, but it also broke the image I had always held of the teacher as godlike.

Studies (Reyes 1978; Philips 1983; Gibson 1988; Trueba 1990a, 1990b) have shown that a student-centered approach may be incongruent with some minority home literacy and language patterns. As a member of a minority myself, I believe that although at first it may be hard for many minority students to engage in this kind of learning, they are fascinated by the notion of equality between teacher and student and appreciate the freedom of expression and choice this approach gives them. They see value in this kind of learning and enjoy the benefits of the new culture, and they try hard to accommodate themselves to what they respect. I do not think teachers should be afraid of doing something incongruent with the ways these students were raised, as every culture has room for improvement and every nation progresses by adopting others' strengths for its own benefit. As long as the ways and values those students are brought up with are not sneered at or held in contempt, they will not feel left out or alienated. To be sensitive to our students' ways of learning, to understand their backgrounds, and to help them reach their goals and dreams will be more helpful and highly appreciated by them than simply leaving them alone.

In the past fifteen years, many studies (Ogbu 1987; Gibson 1987b; Trueba 1990a, 1990b; Finnan, 1987) on ethnic issues tend to categorize minority students into ethnic groups.

Students' behaviors and personalities are attributed to certain cultural values and ethnic characteristics, so that minority students are looked at more as an ethnic species rather than as individual beings. Studies in this field, researched through surveys or case studies, tend to describe the general patterns of behavior of the ethnic group. As a result, ethnic students are stereotyped: Asian students are described as obedient and hardworking, while Black and Mexican-American students are believed to not take school seriously and to give up easily (Ogbu 1974; Gibson 1987b; Trueba, Lila, and Kirton 1990). Little attention is given to individual personalities and experiences. Neglect of the complexity and subtlety of human qualities results in many minority students' being forced to live up to those stereotypes.

Other studies on language learning and on the cultural adjustment of ethnic minority students group those students together and suggest the same kind of teaching strategies for all of them. As Virginia Allen states in her recent study (1991):

> Children whose home language is not English are often lumped together as LEPs, that is, children of Limited English Proficiency. Such a label, although it may seem convenient, tends to support the mistaken belief that these children are a group with similar needs and they can be treated in a similar way. However, their single dimension of likeness, the need to acquire the English language as a second language, is a slim one. On the other hand, the differences among these children are many and have great educational significance. (p. 356)

Many scholars of human development (Vygotsky 1978; Bruner 1986; Gardner 1985) have pointed out that human beings are culturally and historically constructed, but that their personal experience as individuals within the larger culture also shapes their way of doing and seeing things. Bruner (1986) quotes Amelie Rorty in his *Actual Minds, Possible Worlds*:

> We are different entities as we conceive ourselves enlightened by these various views. Our powers of action are different, our relations to one another, our properties and proprieties, our

characteristic success or defeats, our conception of society's proper structures and freedom will vary with our conceptions of ourselves as characters, persons, selves, individuals. (p. 40)

Awareness of individual differences among students will not only help teachers avoid stereotyping, but will also aid them in working out appropriate instructional strategies for individual students. It can help them understand why a certain approach works with some students but not with others, even though they share the same cultural and language backgrounds. My study, which focuses on four Laotian teenagers from one family, highlights the differences as well as the similarities of their individual learning processes. While the similarities reflect their shared cultural and historical background, the differences point to the diversity and complexity of individuals from the same family and culture.

Teaching English to ESL Students

With a focus on the learning experiences of four limited-English-speaking students, my research draws attention to the teaching of English as a second language. Most research on the language learning of students with limited English proficiency has examined the language instruction and the learning patterns of those students in settings and programs separated from mainstream students in regular classrooms. My work focuses more on the learning experience of limited-English-speaking students in mainstream settings. In public schools, whether primary or secondary, programs of teaching English as a second language and bilingual programs serve mainly as transitional programs for limited-English-speaking students to be mainstreamed in regular classrooms. According to Allen (1991), in most districts, "[in] English as a Second Language (ESL) programs, [children are] in the regular classroom setting for most of the day, but [are] pulled out of the classroom to receive special instruction in English as a second language" (p. 361). Every day at school, ESL students like

Tran, Paw, Cham, and Sy spend most of their time in regular classrooms where they study mainstream curricula and are surrounded by native English-speaking peers. In short, the regular classroom represents the mainstream culture to which they have to adjust in their school life.

Penfield (1987) surveyed regular classroom teachers and found that while many of them thought ESL students should be integrated into regular classrooms, such placements created problems, because these teachers did not consider themselves competent to integrate the acquisition of English with the learning of curricular content. My study, with its detailed description of the reading and writing experiences of four ESL students in regular classrooms, complements Penfield's by presenting those students' learning situations from *their* point of view instead of their teachers'.

The Problems of Tracking

Through the specific examples and detailed description of Tran, Paw, and Cham, refugee children tracked at the low level in their school learning, my study typifies the situation of all students ranked at the bottom. These students are bombarded with endless worksheets, surrounded by meaningless mechanical skills and decontextualized spelling words, and suffocated with frequent tests and quizzes. Every day they numbly move disconnected words from books to worksheets and are trained to passively follow the rules. In his study, Goodlad (1984) describes the same situation:

> In English language arts the dominant emphasis throughout was on mechanics—capitalization, punctuation, paragraphs, . . . parts of speech, etc. These were repeated in successive grades of the elementary years, were reviewed in the junior high years, and reappeared in the low-track classes of the senior high schools. (p. 205)

Students in low-track classes are not taught to communicate with words and explore their world through reading and writing, but to memorize, recall, and follow. Consequently they acquire more confusion than knowledge and suffer humiliation more than build confidence in their learning. Though the native-English-speaking students in the low-track classes do not appear to be as silent as Tran, Paw, and Cham, they vent their anger, curse in frustration, and give up on themselves as learners. Worst of all, they set a negative example to students who are new to this culture, who interpret their frustration as the behavior of all American young people. As I saw those angry and confused students, I felt they are perhaps more humiliated than my subjects, whose poor school achievement can be attributed to their limited English skills and their being newcomers to the culture. But what about their American peers? Those students can only blame themselves for being "dumb." At school, my informants feel like outsiders to the culture, while their peers in the same low-level classes might feel like outcasts, rejected insiders.

One of the barriers that hindered Tran, Paw, and Cham's learning is that their schoolwork kept them too busy to talk with others, to take risks, to explore what they knew and could do. Their busywork kept them in the corner, isolated and silenced. The weekly spelling tests, monthly reading quiz, and book reports were on their minds all the time. Tran did not have time to write his stories, as he never had enough time for his "job"; Paw had no time to do her reading and had to determine answers in her tests according to how much time was left. Once Cham had less pressure and more free time, he changed from a "failure" to a different person: he could think, draw, tell stories—he read to learn, wrote to express himself, and worked with imagination and passion.

The questions are: Do students really learn when we keep them busy with endless worksheets and press them with tests? Do we really believe that our students are engaged in learning when we see them rush in and out from class to class? Judging by what Tran, Cham, and Paw did most at school and how they did their work, I do not think so. They spent most of their time memorizing words out of context and taking spelling tests, but a week later they had forgotten most of what they had memorized. They wrote and read things that made little sense to them, and that confused and humiliated them. Instead of filling our students' time with endless mechanical work and quizzes, I think schools should give them more time to think, more opportunities to explore what they want to learn and what they can do, and more space to take risks. Students tracked at the lower level have the least time and space to think, to explore knowledge and take risks. Keeping busy does not mean busywork, and doing meaningless work is wasting everyone's time, energy, and money.

Time, Space, Freedom for Students

Students need not only more time and space, but also more freedom in their learning. They should be instructed to try different ways to learn and to express themselves. Compared with his brothers and sister, Sy was the least prepared for school. But he made the most progress as a reader and writer in the school year when my research was conducted, because he wrote constantly and was given time and help to try different genres to use language and express himself. If, like his brothers and sister, his days had been packed with worksheets and tests, he would most likely have been as much a failure as Cham was in the eleventh-grade English class. If Sy had been required to write book reports like Tran and Paw, then he would have remained as confused as he had been in the reading-discussion period. If Sy's teacher had not allowed him to get help from his sister for his writing or do other writing assignments in his English class at first, he would easily have given up because of unfamiliarity and confusion. He needed more time to try new concepts with more help and at a different pace from his peers. Susan, Sy's English teacher, not only allowed Sy time and flexibility to explore new territory in his learning, but also gave herself opportunities to understand a student like Sy.

The fact that Sy was the one of my four informants who had benfitted most from his schooling in that year shows that high-school education in the United States is much more rigid than middle- and primary-school education. High schools have an extremely prescribed curriculum. There is also considerable pressure from both administrators and parents to prepare students for college. Teachers in high schools worry about their students' SAT scores more than their students do. Critical essays and classic literature are considered the only appropriate content for high-school English. Of course, for students like Tran, Cham, and Paw, this can be a problem. With the rigid curriculum, it is impossible for them to succeed on a high-school level until their language skills have developed and the knowledge base required by the high-school curriculum has been acquired. Many high-school teachers share Cham's eleventh-grade English teacher's frustration with placement of such students at a high-school level with such low language ability.

If we teach for a set standard or our teaching is bound by a prescribed curriculum, students like Tran, Paw, and Cham can never be included in mainstream classrooms. Only when we care about our students' real learning, instead of pressing them to do work at a certain level, will we really help them to learn. Dewey (1902) advised teachers to find out what children needed instead of forcing them to read materials that the teachers think are good for them. In a discussion of high-school teaching, Powell, Farrar, and Cohen (1985) explain: "Dewey and others had urged educators to remake the curriculum so that it exploited students' natural curiosity, responded to their real-life interests, and encouraged them to make choices about what to study and how" (p. 258).

Cham's learning experiences in two different English classes have demonstrated that students like Cham will fail when we make them work but not learn, and students can learn when we teach to their interests and care for their real learning. Cham's eleventh-grade English teacher tried to give her students what they lacked (language skills and vocabulary) and made them work hard by administering frequent tests and quizzes. Cham worked very hard every day, but he rarely understood his work and soon forgot most of what he tried to memorize. In contrast, Cham's tenth-grade English teacher taught more to his students' interests. Instead of giving tests, he let his students write what they wanted to know and express. In that class, Cham read more, wrote more, and understood what he read and wrote. He improved more in his language learning in six weeks in the tenth-grade English class than he had in six months in his eleventh-grade English class. The fundamental differences between Cham's two English teachers are that one saw what her students lacked, while the other what his students could do; one focused on curriculum, while the other focused on the students. If we could assess our students' progress according to how much they individually gain in a year instead of by certain set standards, we would do much better in our teaching. Because of their lack of language skills and education, Tran, Paw, and Cham will never succeed at the high-school level by traditional standards. But if each year we could judge school success based on each learner's improvement, students like Tran, Paw, and Cham would be much better off. Cham certainly had achieved success in his second English class, though he was still far behind most of his peers in reading and writing.

Of course, it is unfair simply to blame high schools for their obsession with tests and curriculum. In his recent open letter to the President of Harvard University, Steve Seidel (1994) advocates: "if [we] want K–12 education to change in profound ways, higher education may have to change in pro-found ways" (p. 1). If SAT scores continue to be a main criterion for college admission, we should not blame high schools for their tracking students and teaching for tests and certain set standards instead of concentrating on individual learners and whole persons. We have to admit the fact that higher education and its standards for admission greatly affect the structure of the high-school curriculum and its approach to assessment. If higher education keeps its traditional admission requirements, it will be hard for high-school education to reform in profound ways.

I have focused my attention on four individuals for almost two years. In writing about them, I entangled myself in their situations, their experiences and emotions. Sometimes I could not tell whether I was describing their situation or representing them as their attorney. By writing about them, I felt close to them, even closer than when I was with them physically. Many times I could identify with them, sympathize with them, and understand their pain and frustration, triumphs and joy from my personal experiences as a learner in the new culture. I know if I were trapped as they were in those lower-level classes and buried with endless tests and meaningless basic skill work, I would do no better than they. I am confident if they are given the opportunity and freedom to learn, to connect, and to explore in their learning as I was free to do in my doctoral program, they will excel.

The closer I looked at my informants, the more I found they had great potential as readers and writers. When our children come to school, they do not come in a vacuum. They carry their home culture and literary and life experiences with them. They come to us full of curiosity and imagination. Students like Tran, Paw, Cham, and Sy come to us with unusual backgrounds and experiences. They are filled with hopes and dreams, and also questions and wonders. What each of our students carries with him or her should be the resource for our teaching as well as the starting point of the student's learning. Imagine if Tran, Paw, and Cham had been given the chance to share their stories and their past experiences with their classmates in their reading and writing activities, how much we and our students would learn from them, and how much their stories would enrich our understanding of our world and those who have had a life different from ours! If we let Tran, Paw, and Cham write about themselves and read to find out what they want to know, their reading and writing would make sense to them and also help them understand the world they came to join.

If we let them hear more from their American peers, they would better understand the nation they want to be part of. In expressing what they know and inquiring about what they want to know in their reading and writing, they would learn to use the language to master skills and to expand their vocabulary. Then we could introduce them to more unfamiliar territory and help them communicate their understanding of new knowledge with a higher level of proficiency. Totally ignoring what our students can do and want to learn, but just teaching what we have to cover is not truly teaching, but "dumping."

The problems my informants were confronted with at school cannot be blamed on their linguistic code, their cultural backgrounds, or their different ways of learning, all of which are often considered the major hindrances to learning for students such as these. The source of students' problems in school is not to be found in the students themselves, but, as Mehan, Hertwick, and Meihls (1986) argue,

> it is to be found in the organization of the school. The problems that lower class and ethnic children face in school must be viewed as a consequence of institutional arrangements which ensnare children, by not being sensitive to the fact that children display skills differently in different situations. (p. 123)

Institutional arrangements also enslave learners with what the school has to cover and impose upon them what it thinks they need, ignoring their values, their needs, their interests, their intelligence, and their ways of knowing. The typical schedule for schools in this country (especially at the high-school level, with five minutes between classes and half an hour for lunch) and its curriculum (limited by certain scope and sequence) fails to give our students time, space, freedom, and flexibility to explore, to take risks, and to think and imagine. Students are treated as empty bottles to fill up and robots to be drilled and trained rather than resourceful, intelligent beings with feelings and emotions. Education

should be for the purpose of developing students' intellectual power and treating them as individuals with richly varied
possibilities.

Time, Flexibility, Control for Teachers

I have presented my informants' experiences in specific classrooms with specific examples from their perspective, and this
may have made certain teachers appear to be victimizers of the
students, or the cause of their disconnected and disengaged
learning. Actually, I do not intend to make teachers the target.
I believe they are the scapegoats of the system and themselves
victims of the school structure. Every day they are exhausted
by what they have to cover, although they know their students
may have little interest in what they are required to do. They
have little freedom or control over what to teach and how to
arrange daily or yearly schedules. To help students get
through school, they have to teach for tests and prepare students for good grades. Like their own students, they do not
have time to learn from books, from their students, or from
their colleagues; they can only rush through the teaching
requirements set by the institution. Tangled by the system,
they try hard to survive day by day at school themselves. As a
participant-researcher in school, I experienced personally the
frustration of being a teacher who could not help students
learn, but only help them rush through the requirements. The
detrimental thing to our students is not so much what we
teachers cannot do for them as it is our being blindly driven
to do what we are required to do, without questioning what
we are doing.

In order for teachers to improve their teaching, they must
be given more time, flexibility, and control in their profession.
A monthly half-day workshop for staff development is usually
used to catch up on what is mandated from the top or fash-
ioned in the field. That is sometimes more confusing and over-
whelming than helpful to teachers. They need time to read, to
visit their colleagues' classrooms, to observe different levels of

teaching, and to simply chat with people in the building and in the neighborhood. The conflict between Paw and Cham's ESL teacher and their English teacher shown reflects the lack of communication and collaboration among teachers. If we teachers are unable to collaborate with or learn from each other, how can we require our students to do so? If a school is not a literate community for teachers, how can it be for our students? Teachers have served as role models in every generation and culture, but we need to practice what we preach.

School structure is at fault, but no structure can be changed overnight. Reconstruction of a system takes generations because people who set out to change a structure should first become conscious of their own existence, examine their situation, and question the status quo. Only when they start to feel the pain and constraint caused by the old structure can they start to think of change. However, we are all born into a set system and easily take for granted what it is. We take what we inherit and pass it on to the next generation without questioning, no matter how frustrated and overwhelmed we are with it. That is why change takes time. It is a process of deconstruction and reconstruction that requires us to look at our world with a new perspective and loosen our bonds with old habits. Once we realize the cause of our constraint and discomfort, we can make changes. First, we must take control of our everyday lives and make small changes in our immediate world, the classroom. Every bit of effort we make contributes to the construction of a new system or a completion of our world. Pragmatists hold that our world is in the process of forming, so every one of us who believes in change and in bettering our world for future generations should contribute to this process of perfection.

A Multicultural Approach

This book has examined the learning experiences of four students with limited English proficiency (LEP) in regular classrooms. But the issues I have dealt with concern not only the problems of mainstreaming LEP students like Tran, Paw, Cham, and Sy and the teaching of students at the low-track levels, but also the nature of reading and writing instruction in multicultural settings. Demographers estimate that by the year 2000 one of every three children in the United States will be from minority groups. To face the social needs of a pluralistic society, American schools should prepare children with different cultural backgrounds to work and live together as one nation. To achieve this purpose, as cultural theorists (Trueba 1987, 1988b, 1989; Tharp and Gallimore 1989; Spindler and Spindler 1987) suggest, teachers of all subjects should create classrooms that are culturally congruent environments for students to integrate their cultural values into literacy learning. Multiculturalism has become a hot topic these days. We hear of everything from multicultural books, projects, and units to celebrations of Black History Month and the Jewish or Chinese New Year. Publishers of basals are doing a good job catching up with the fashion.

However, it seems that multiculturalism is interpreted not as multiple cultures but as cultures other than the dominant one. It bothers me when I hear many people say, "We cover multiculturalism. We had a unit on Japan [or China or Africa]" or "We've read Native American stories, books with black people and the folklore of Russia and France." Except for those isolated activities, they keep the same agenda and use the same approach as they always did in their literacy instruction.

Multiculturalism really means an inclusion and an embrace of every one of us under the umbrella of democracy. It does not mean getting rid of whiteness or adding other colors as decoration to the curriculum. It means recognizing, valuing, and empowering every one of our students in their learning, no matter what color they are, what backgrounds they come from, or what language they speak at home. White people are not all the same, just as not all black people are good at sports and music and not all Asians are quiet, obedient, and hardworking. One of the points I attempt to make in this book is that humans are too complicated to be grouped as stereotypes. Even from the same family, my four informants are different. Tran longs for a leadership role; Cham dreams of becoming rich; Paw desires a good relationship; and Sy is simply thrilled to become an eighth grader. They have much in common, yet they are different in many ways because of each of their unique personalities and life experiences.

A multicultural approach does not mean simply adopting a week-long unit on China or India around the holidays, or a month's unit on black history. It must include every student's voice in every subject we teach every day. By inviting students to share their own stories or express their interpretations of their reading, teachers not only allow students to construct knowledge and make meaning in their reading and writing, but also enable them to share their perspectives and cultural values. In this way, teaching cultivates in the young an appreciation of differences, a respect for individuality and a way of looking at the world with plural meanings. Through interaction, students can learn language in meaningful contexts and for real communication, and they can also learn the art of negotiation of meaning through recognizing each other's voice and values. In Bruner's words (1986), "Negotiation is the art of constructing new meaning in which individuals can regulate their relations with each other" (p. 149). Students should have an opportunity to listen to speakers of different cultures and to visit different communities. Without personal contact or hearing words directly from the speakers of other cultures, it is hard to appreciate the beauty of words or values and images simply from books. We have to remember that every one of us carries our home culture and literacy with us. Thus, multiculture is not cultures other than white, but cultures of the nation.

But multiculturalism does not mean that America as a multicultural, multiracial country has no uniform beliefs and values. The fundamental principles of this democratic society are freedom, equality, and individuality. These qualities are what people all over the world have come, and continue to come, to this country to seek. Freire and Macedo (1987) hold that "literacy and education in general are cultural expressions" (p. 51). The purpose of formal schooling is to familiarize the young with the fundamental cultural values of a society. In addition to the teaching materials, which are used as the major means to introduce cultural values to students, a school's teaching approach should also demonstrate cultural values. In a democratic society such as the United States, classrooms should be places where students can experience democratic social values in their literacy learning.

It is devastating to see the children of immigrants like Cham, who only associate America with money and whose search for freedom, equality, and individuality is fading into dreams only of becoming rich. There is nothing wrong with pursuing a better life, but many immigrants have sacrificed so much, even their lives, for more than simply a material success in this country. From the early Pilgrims to recent refugees who gaze at the Statue of Liberty, all newcomers to this country are inspired to feel spiritual liberty, a sense of freedom, and a feeling of self-worth. Every one of them knew that it was not easy to leave everything behind and start all over again in a strange land, but they were willing to make sacrifices for democratic values and for the chance that their children might have a better life than they had before. Trueba, Lila, and Kirton (1990) state:

> Without the contributions, loyalty and extraordinary energy of the incessant waves of immigrants from all over the world, American democracy would have long ceased to exist. Immigrants and refugees come to America searching for economic opportunities and political and religious freedom, "The American Dream." No one else knows better than the immigrants and refugees the meaning of freedom and democracy, and no one is willing to pay a higher price in order to achieve the American dream. Therefore they endure hardships and drastic social and cultural changes unbearable for others, and they buy into American ideals and social, economic and political participation, and of educational opportunity equally

accessible to all. Indeed they learn that the very foundations of American democratic institutions are linked to the reality of ethnic diversity and the eager dedication of newcomers to succeed. (p. 1)

All our teachers need to inculcate in all their students genuine appreciation for the richness of American culture. The democratic values of freedom, equality, and individuality should be integrated into instructional models. Students should be introduced to the values of freedom and individuality in class by being given the freedom to choose their own reading and writing, to discover what they want to find out, and to speak in their own voice. Instead of tracking students into ranked groups, making them feel either superior or inferior to others, we should encourage them to understand, respect, and work with each other in their school community. Each individual contributes to meaning-making in his or her literacy learning. We should consciously create our classrooms as communities in which people learn to work together, and accept the fact that people learn differently and have different ways of knowing. Today, in classrooms, we should let our students experience democratic values in order to prepare them for their lives tomorrow in a democratic world.

Epilogue

I collected the data for this study in 1990 and 1991. The stories told in this book all happened that year. But what became of the young people after they graduated from the high school? What are they doing now?

In June 1992, Tran, Paw, and Cham graduated from high school. I was invited to their graduation and joined them for the pictures and reception afterward. That was a moment of jubilation, with every member of the Savang family at the school ground. In September of that year, all three high-school graduates were enrolled in a two-year technology institute in a town not far from their home. Tran majored in computer drafting, Paw in a nursing program, and Cham in mechanical engineering. They received scholarships and loans to help them pay their own way through the college. As Mr. Savang said, "I have so many children, I can't afford to send them all to college. They have to pay for their own education."

Two years later, Tran graduated from the college and received an AS (associate degree in science) in computer drafting. He now works in an immigration office, computer-processing visa applications. He is very happy with his job. He wants to continue his education in a four-year college, but he needs to make some money first.

After one year as a full-time student in the technology institute, Paw became a part-time student, as she had to work thirty-five hours a week in a nursing home. Now she is thinking about changing her major and getting a degree in accounting. She still lives at home and takes on as much housework responsibility as she can. She still likes to read and write. When she knew I was preparing this book, she asked to have a copy.

Cham has a full-time job in an auto-parts factory. He takes one course each semester in the institute, but is not sure whether he is going to get a college degree or not. He still dreams of making enough money for a trip back to Laos. Cham is the handyman in the house. He takes care of the carpentry work around the house and has built sheds for the chickens, rabbits, ducks, and geese in their backyard.

Sy is going to be a junior in high school. He is still quiet and does not have friends, although he participates in school activities and is considered one of the best players on the school soccer team. He seldom reads or writes unless he has to for school. Jane, his ESL teacher, thinks his best year was his seventh-grade year with Susan. In Jane's words, "He read and wrote so much that year, and felt good about himself too. Now he rarely reads. When I told him that I found some books for him to read in the summer, he showed no interest and never came to get them." Sy has already made up his mind that he will not go to college. He thinks college would be too hard for him.

The Savang family still lives at the same place. Mr. Savang and his two older sons still work in a medical technology factory from 7 A.M. to 7 P.M. three days a week, and Mrs. Savang and one of the older daughters continue to work in the seafood plant in a nearby town. They feel lucky that none of them lost their jobs, even at a time when the unemployment rate was very high in their state. They feel their life is getting better since the younger children who used to be in school started working. Most of the children still live at home, except Tran, who moved to live with one of the sisters in Massachusetts. As before, the children living at home give half of their monthly paycheck to their father and keep the other half for themselves.

The biggest change in the family concerns Mei, the older daughter whom I took to the indoor swimming pool. Mei is engaged to an American man, who happens to be the son of one of my very close friends. During the year of my research, I introduced this young man to Tran after Tran told me that he wanted to meet Americans, but that it was so hard to make friends with them at school. Tran and this American young man did become good friends. As their friendship developed, this American young man became close to other members of the family.

I am glad to see this intercultural marriage happening in the Savang house. I am sure this young man is going to become a person that the family can depend on, to help them understand more of their new culture and interpret for them the complexity of the new world. He will also help his American family and friends understand and appreciate people like the Savangs. This intercultural marriage not only represents the integration of cultures and people of different races, but it also shows that once people get to know each other, despite their differences they can accommodate one another and become one family under one roof.

I also feel good about this intercultural marriage, as its being one of the results of my research. Through my research, the Savangs opened their door not only to me, a person who is very much like them, but also to more Americans, people who are different from them. This openness will lead to a depth of understanding, appreciation, and respect of two different cultures and ethnic groups and will contribute to the unity of our nation of immigrants.

As for my own story, I have continued my career in this country. After I graduated from my doctoral program, I took a teaching position at Towson State University in Maryland. I constantly share my own stories and stories of the people I have studied with my undergraduate and graduate students as well as my colleagues. I will continue to learn and grow as a professional in my new culture. Although many times I still feel overwhelmed and frustrated as an outsider in this culture, I can handle it better because I now understand that all growth involves both pain and joy.

Bibliography

Agar, M. H. 1980. *The Professional Stranger: An Informal Introduction to Ethnography*. New York: Academic Press.

Allen, V. G. 1991. "Teaching Bilingual and ESL Children." In *Handbook of Research on Teaching the English Language Arts*, ed. J. Flood et al. New York: Macmillan.

Applebee, A., J. Langer, and I. Mullis. 1987. *Learning to Be Literate in America: Reading, Writing, and Reasoning*. Princeton, NJ: Educational Testing Service.

————. 1991. "Environments for Language Teaching and Learning: Contemporary Issues and Future Directions." In *Handbook of Research on Teaching the English Language Arts*, ed. J. Flood et al. New York: Macmillan.

Asher, Carol. 1989. "Southeast Asian Adolescents: Identity and Adjustment." Review in *ERIC/CUE Digest*, No. 51. New York: ERIC Clearinghouse on Urban Education.

Atwell, N. 1987. *In the Middle: Writing, Reading, and Learning with Adolescents*. Portsmouth, NH: Boynton/Cook–Heinemann.

Au, K., and C. Jordan. 1981. "Teaching Reading to Hawaiian Children: Finding a Culturally Appropriate Solution." In *Culture and the Bilingual Classrooms*, ed. H. Trueba, G. Guthrie, and K. Au. Rowley, MA: Newbury House.

Baumann, J., and E. Kameenui. 1991. "Research on Vocabulary Instruction: Ode to Voltaire." In *Handbook of Research on Teaching the English Language Arts*, ed. J. Flood et al. New York: Macmillan.

Beck, L., E. McCaslin, and M. McKeown. 1980. *The Rationale and Design of a Program to Teach Vocabulary to Fourth-grade Students*. Pittsburgh, PA: University of Pittsburgh, Learning Research and Development Center.

Belenky, M., B. Clinchy, N. Goldberger, and J. Tarule. 1986. *Women's Ways of Knowing*. New York: Basic Books.

Bennett, P. 1991. "Welcome to L.A." *The Boston Globe*. Special issue on multiculturalism. October.

Berthoff, A. 1981. *The Making of Meaning: Metaphors, Models, and Maxims for Writing Teachers*. Portsmouth, NH: Boynton/ Cook–Heinemann.

Bidwell, C., and N. Friedkin. 1988. "The Sociology of Education." In *The Handbook of Sociology*, ed. N. Smelser. Newbury Park, CA: Sage Publications.

Blakely, M. 1982a. "American Talking . . . Listen! How some Hmong, Khmer, Lao and Vietnamese View American Schools." Paper presented at the conference "Options: Bridge to English."

———. 1982b. "Southeast Asian Refugee Parent Survey." Paper presented at the Conference of the Oregon Educational Research Association.

———. 1983. "Southeast Asian Refugee Parents: An Inquiry into Home-School Communication and Understanding." *Anthropology and Education Quarterly* 14 (1) (Spring): 43–68.

———. 1989. "Instructional Strategies for Limited English Students." *New Focus*. The National Clearinghouse for Bilingual Education Occasional Papers in Bilingual Education. October 20.

Bolinger, D. 1980. *Language: The Loaded Weapon*. New York: Longman.

Boyer, E. 1983. *High School: A Report on Secondary Education in America*. New York: Harper and Row.

Britton, J. 1971. "What's the Use? A Schematic Account of Language Functions." *Educational Review* 23 (1): 205–19.

———. 1972. *Language and Learning*. Harmondsworth, England: Penguin Books.

Britton, J., T. Burgess, N. Martin, A. Mcleod, and H. Rosen. 1975. *The Development of Writing Abilities*. London: Macmillan Educational for the School Council.

Britton, J., and M. Chorny. 1991. "Current Issues and Future Directions." In *Handbook of Research on Teaching the English Language Arts*, ed. J. Flood et al. New York: Macmillan.

Brown, R. 1991. *Schools of Thought*. San Francisco, CA: Jossey-Bass.

Bruner, J. 1979. *On Knowing*. Cambridge, MA: Harvard University Press.

————. 1986. *Actual Minds, Possible Worlds*. Cambridge, MA: Harvard University Press.

————. 1990. *Acts of Meaning*. Cambridge, MA: Harvard University Press.

Caplan, N., M. Choy, and J. Whitmore. 1991. *Children of the Boat People: A Study of Educational Success*. Ann Arbor: University of Michigan Press.

Chan, I. 1981. "The Hmong in America—Their Cultural Continuities and Discontinuities." St. Paul, MN: Bush Foundation.

Coles, R. 1989. *The Call of Stories*. Boston, MA: Houghton Mifflin.

Cook-Gumperz, J., ed. 1986. *The Social Construction of Literacy*. New York: Cambridge University Press.

Courts, P. 1991. *Literacy and Empowerment: The Meaning Makers*. New York: Bergin & Garvey.

Cummins, J. 1986. "Empowering Minority Students: A Framework for Intervention." *Harvard Educational Review* 56 (5): 18–36.

Delgado-Gaitan, C. 1987. "Traditions and Transitions in the Learning Process of Mexican Children: An Ethnographic View." In *Interpretive Ethnography of Education: At Home and Abroad*, ed. G. Spindler and L. Spindler. Hillsdale, NJ: Lawrence Erlbaum Associates.

Delgado-Gaitan, C., and H. Trueba. 1991. *Crossing Cultural Borders*. New York: Falmer Press.

Delpit, L. 1988. "The Silenced Dialogue: Power and Pedagogy in Educating Other People's Children." *Harvard Educational Review* 5 (3): 280–98.

Dewey, J. [1902] 1956. *The Child and the Curriculum/The School and Society*. Chicago: University of Chicago Press.

————. [1938] 1963. *Experience and Education*. New York: Macmillan.

————. [1916] 1966. *Democracy and Education*. New York: The Free Press.

Donaldson, M. 1978. *Children's Minds*. New York: W. W. Norton & Co.

Eagleton, T. 1976. *Marxism and Literacy Criticism*. Berkeley, CA: University of California Press.

Edwards, J. 1985. *Language, Society and Identity*. New York: Basil Blackwell.

Elbow, P. 1973. *Writing without Teachers*. New York: Oxford University Press.

Emig, J. 1983. *The Web of Meaning: Essays on Writing, Teaching, Learning, and Thinking*, ed. D. Gaswami and M. Butler. Portsmouth, NH: Boynton/Cook–Heinemann.

Erickson, F. 1982. "Taught Cognitive Learning in Its Immediate Environments: A Neglected Topic in the Anthropology of Education." *Anthropology and Education Quarterly* 13 (2): 149–80.

————. 1987. "Transformation and School Success: The Politics and Culture of Educational Achievement." *Anthropology and Education Quarterly* 18 (4): 335–56.

Farr, M. 1991. "Dialects, Culture, and Teaching the English Language Arts." In *Handbook of Research on Teaching the English Language Arts*, eds. J. Flood et al. New York: Macmillan.

Farrell, E. 1991. "Instructional Models For English Language Arts, K–12." In *Handbook of Research on Teaching the English Language Arts*, eds. J. Flood et al. New York: Macmillan.

Finnan, C. R. 1987. "The Influence of the Ethnic Community on the Adjustment of Vietnamese Refugees." In *Interpretive Ethnography of Education: At Home and Abroad*, ed. G. Spindler and L. Spindler. Hillsdale, NJ: Lawrence Erlbaum Associates.

Fish, S. 1980. *Is There a Text in This Class? The Authority of Interpretive Communities*. Cambridge, MA: Harvard University Press.

Fishman, A. 1988. *Amish Literacy: What and How It Means*. Portsmouth, NH: Heinemann.

Fletcher, R. 1991. *Walking Trees: Teaching Teachers in the New York City Schools*. Portsmouth, NH: Heinemann.

Flood, J., J. Jensen, D. Lapp, and J. Squire, eds. 1991. *Handbook of Research on Teaching the English Language Arts*. New York: Macmillan.

Freire, P. 1970. *Pedagogy of the Oppressed*. New York: Seabury Press.

———. 1985. *The Politics of Education: Culture, Power and Liberation*. South Hadley, MA: Bergin & Garvey.

Freire, P., and F. Macedo. 1987. "Literacy: Reading the Word and the World." In *The Critical Studies in Education Series*, ed. P. Freire and H. Ciroux. South Hadley, MA: Bergin & Garvey.

Garcia, S., and A. Ortiz. 1989. "Preventing Inappropriate Referrals of Language Minority Students to Special Education." *New Focus*. The National Clearinghouse for Bilingual Education Occasional Papers in Bilingual Education. October 20.

Gardner, H. 1985. *Frames of Mind*. New York: Basic Books.

Geertz, C. 1973. *The Interpretation of Cultures*. New York: Basic Books.

Gibson, M. 1987a. "Playing by the Rules." In *Education and Cultural Process*, 2nd. ed., ed. G. Spindler. Prospect Heights, IL: Waveland.

———. 1987b. "The School Performance of Immigrant Minorities: A Comparative View." *Anthropology and Education Quarterly* 18 (4): 262–75.

———. 1988. *Accommodation without Assimilation: Punjabi Sikh Immigrants in an American High School and Community*. Ithaca, New York: Cornell University Press.

Goleman, J. 1986. "The Dialogic Imagination: More Than We've Been Taught." In *Only Connect*, ed. T. Newkirk. Portsmouth, NH: Boynton/Cook–Heinemann.

Goodlad, J. 1984. *A Place Called School: Prospects for the Future*. New York: McGraw-Hill.

Goodman, K. 1986. *What's Whole in Whole Language*. Portsmouth, NH: Heinemann.

Goodman, K., and Y. Goodman. 1978. "Reading of American Children Whose Language Is a Stable Rural Dialect of English or a Language Other Than English." Washington, DC: U.S. Department of Health, Education, and Welfare.

Graham, R. 1991. "Myth of Migration." *The Boston Globe*. October 13.

Graves, D. 1983. *Writing: Teachers and Children at Work*. Portsmouth, NH: Heinemann.

———. 1985. "All Children Can Write." *Learning Disabilities Focus* 1(2): 36–43.

———. 1991. *Build a Literate Classroom*. Portsmouth, NH: Heinemann.

Graves, D., and B. Sunstein, eds. 1992. *Portfolio Portraits*. Portsmouth, NH: Heinemann.

Greene, M. 1988. *The Dialectic of Freedom*. New York: Teachers College Press.

Hansen, J. 1987. *When Writers Read*. Portsmouth, NH: Heinemann.

Hansen, J., and D. Graves. 1991. "Unifying the English Language Arts Curriculum: The Language Arts Interact." In *Handbook of Research on Teaching the English Language Arts*, ed. J. Flood et al. New York: Macmillan.

Hansen, J., T. Newkirk, and D. Graves, eds. 1985. *Breaking New Ground: Teachers Relate Reading and Writing in the Elementary School*. Portsmouth, NH: Heinemann.

Harmon, R. 1979. "Understanding Laotian People, Language, and Culture." *Bilingual Education Resource Series*. Olympia, WA:

Washington Office of the State Superintendent of Public Instruction.

Harste, J., V. Woodward, and C. Burke. 1984. *Language Stories and Literacy Lessons*. Portsmouth, NH: Heinemann.

Heath, S. B. 1983. *Ways with Words: Language, Life, and Work in Communities and Classrooms*. New York: Cambridge University Press.

Henry IV, W. H. 1990. "Beyond the Melting Pot." *New York Times*. April 9.

Hubbard, R. 1989. *Authors of Pictures, Draughtsmen of Words*. Portsmouth, NH: Heinemann.

Hunter, W., and L. Nguyen. 1977. *Educational Systems in South Vietnam and of Southeast Asians in Comparison with Educational Systems in the United States*. Ames: Iowa State University.

James, W. 1968. *Pragmatism*. New York: Meridian Books.

John-Steiner, V. 1985. *Notebooks of the Mind*. New York: Harper and Row.

Kameenui, E., D. Dixon, and R. Carnine. 1987. "Issues in the Design of Vocabulary Instruction." In *The Nature of Vocabulary Acquisition*, ed. M. McKeown and M. Curtis. Hillsdale, NJ: Lawrence Erlbaum Associates.

Khleif, B. 1978. "Insiders, Outsiders, and Renegades: Toward a Classification of Ethnolinguistic Labels." In *Language and Ethnic Relations*, ed. H. Giles and B. St. Jacques.

Lefevre, K. B. 1987. *Invention as a Social Act*. Carbondale, IL: Southern Illinois University Press.

Loth, R. 1991. "The Big New Mix." *The Boston Globe*. October 13.

Maanen, V. 1988. *Tales of the Field: On Writing Ethnography*. Chicago: University of Chicago Press.

Macias, J. 1987. "The Hidden Curriculum of Papago Teachers: American Indian Strategies for Mitigating Cultural Discontinuity in Early Schooling." In *Interpretive Ethnography of Education: At Home and Abroad*, ed. G. Spindler and L. Spindler. Hillsdale, NJ: Lawrence Erlbaum Associates.

MacLure, M. 1988. "Introduction Oracy: Current Trends in Context." In *Oracy Matters*, ed. M. MacLure, T. Phillips, and A. Wilkinson. Philadelphia, PA: Open University Press.

Mehan, H., A. Hertwick, and J. L. Meihls. 1986. *Handicapping the Handicapped: Decision Making in Students' Educational Careers.* Stanford, CA: Stanford University Press.

Moffett, J. 1968. *A Student-Centered Language-Arts Curriculum, Grades K–13: A Handbook for Teachers.* Boston: Houghton Mifflin.

————. 1985. "Hidden Impediments to Improving English Reading." *Phi Delta Kappan* 67 (1): p. 50–56.

————, ed. 1973. *Interaction: A Student-Centered Arts and Reading Program.* Boston: Houghton Mifflin.

Murray, D. 1986. *Read to Write.* New York: Holt, Rinehart and Winston.

————. 1987. *Write to Learn.* New York: Holt, Rinehart and Winston.

————. 1989. *Expecting the Unexpected: Teaching Myself—and Others—to Read and Write.* Portsmouth, NH: Boynton/Cook–Heinemann.

Neilsen, L. 1989. *Literacy and Living: The Literate Lives of Three Adults.* Portsmouth, NH: Heinemann.

Newkirk, T. 1989. *More Than Stories: The Range of Children's Writing.* Portsmouth, NH: Heinemann.

————. 1991. "The High School Years." In *Handbook of Research on Teaching the English Language Arts*, ed. J. Flood et al. New York: Macmillan.

————, ed. 1986a. *Only Connect: Uniting Reading and Writing.* Portsmouth, NH: Boynton/Cook–Heinemann.

————. 1986b. *To Compose: Teaching Writing in the High School.* Portsmouth, NH: Heinemann.

Nguyen, L-D. 1985. "Indochinese Cross-Cultural Adjustment and Communication." Paper presented at the Annual Meeting of the Teachers of English to Other Languages. Houston, TX. March.

Oakes, J. 1985. *Keeping Track: How Schools Structure Inequality.* New Haven, CT: Yale University Press.

Ogbu, J. 1974. *The Next Generation.* New York: Academic Press.

————. 1978. *Minority Education and Caste: The American System in Cross-Cultural Perspective.* New York: Academic Press.

————. 1983. "Minority Status and Schooling in Plural Societies." *Anthropology and Education Review* 27 (2): 168–90.

————. 1987. "Variability in Minority School Performance: A Problem in Search of an Education." *Anthropology and Education Quarterly* 18 (4): 312–14.

Papa, I. 1989. *Turning Points.* New York: Addison-Wesley.

Page, R. 1987. "Lower-Track Classes at a College-Preparatory High School: A Caricature of Education Encounters." In *Interpretive Ethnography of Education: At Home and Abroad,* ed. G. Spindler and L. Spindler. Hillsdale, NJ: Lawrence Erlbaum Associates.

Patel, D. 1988. "Asian Americans: A Growing Force." *The Journal of State Government* (March/April): 71–76.

Penfield, J. 1987. "ESL: The Regular Classroom Teacher's Perspective." *TESOL Quarterly* 21 (1): 21–40.

Philips, S. 1983. *The Invisible Culture.* New York: Longman.

Pinnell, G., and A. Jaggar. 1991. "Oral Language: Speaking and Listening in the Classroom." In *Handbook of Research on Teaching the English Language Arts,* ed. J. Flood et al. New York: Macmillan.

Powell, A., E. Farrar, and D. Cohen. 1985. *The Shopping Mall High School.* Boston, MA: Houghton Mifflin.

Power, B. M., and R. Hubbard, eds. 1991. *Literacy in Process: The Heinemann Reader.* Portsmouth, NH: Heinemann.

Probst, R. E. 1984. *Adolescent Literature: Response and Analysis.* Columbus, OH: Charles E. Merill.

Proudfoot, R. 1990. *Even Birds Don't Sound the Same Here: Laotian Refugees Search for Heart in the American Culture.* New York: Peterlang.

Raizerman, M., and G. Herdricks. 1988. "A Study of Southeast Asian Refugee Youth in the Twin Cities of Minneapolis and St. Paul, Minnesota." Final Report. Southeast Asian Studies, University of Minnesota.

Refugee Service Center. 1981. *The Peoples and Cultures of Cambodia, Laos, and Vietnam.* Washington, DC: Center for Applied Linguistics.

———. 1986. "Resettlement Case Study: Non-Impacted Small Midwestern City." Washington, DC: Center for Applied Linguistics.

———. 1987. "Resettlement Case Study: Young Adults: 17–22 Years Old." Washington, DC: Department of State, Bureau of Refugee Programs.

Reyes, V. 1978. *Bicultural-Bilingual Education for Latino Studies.* New York: Arno Press.

Rigg, P. 1986. "Reading in ESL: Learning from Kids." In *Children with ESL: Integrating Perspectives,* ed. P. Rigg and D. Enright. Washington, DC: Teachers of English to Speakers of Other Languages.

Rober, S., and G. Ward. 1987. "Becoming Marginal." In *Success or Failure? Learning and the Language Minority Students,* ed. H. Trueba. Cambridge, MA: Newbury House.

Rodriguez, R. 1981. *Hunger of Memory.* Boston: David R. Godine.

Rose, M. 1989. *Lives on the Boundary.* New York: Penguin Books.

Rosenblatt, L. 1978. *The Reader, the Text, the Poem.* Carbondale, IL: Southern Illinois University Press.

———. 1983. *Literature as Exploration.* New York: Appleton-Century.

Rubin, D. L. 1985. "Instruction in Speaking and Listening Battles and Options." *Educational Leadership* 42 (1): 31–36.

Rupp, J. 1980. "Attitude and Expectations of Indochinese Parents." Paper presented at the National Conference on Indochinese Education and Social Service. Arlington, VA: March.

Seidel, S. 1994. "How to Change Our Schools in Just One Day." *Harvard Education Letter*. March–April.

Sesser, S. 1990. "A Reporter at Large: Forgotten Country." *New Yorker*. August 20.

Shannon, P. 1990. *The Struggle to Continue: Progressive Reading Instruction in the United States*. Portsmouth, NH: Heinemann.

Sinclair, R., and W. Ghory. 1987. "Becoming Marginal." In *Success or Failure? Learning and the Language Minority Students*, ed. H. Trueba. Cambridge, MA: Newbury House.

Sivell, J., and L. Curtis, eds. 1990. *TESOL '90: Reading into the Future*. Toronto, Canada. Proceedings of the 1990 TESOL Ontario Conference.

Sizer, T. 1984. *Horace's Compromise: The Dilemma of the American High School*. Boston, MA: Houghton Mifflin.

Smith, F. 1982. *Writing and the Writer*. New York: Holt, Rinehart and Winston.

———. 1986. *Insult to Intelligence: The Bureaucratic Invasion of Our Classrooms*. New York: Arbor House.

———. 1988. *Joining the Literacy Club: Further Essays into Education*. Portsmouth, NH: Heinemann.

Smith-Hefner, N. 1990. "Language and Identity in the Education of Boston-Area Khmer." *Anthropology & Education Quarterly*, Vol. 21, No. 3, September.

Spindler, G., and L. Spindler. 1982. "Roger Harker and Schoenhausen: From Familiar to Strange and Back Again." In *Doing the Ethnography of Schooling: Educational Anthropology in Action*, ed. G. Spindler. New York: Holt, Rinehart and Winston.

———. 1983. "Anthropologists' View of American Culture." *Annual Review of Anthropology* 12 (2): 49–78.

———. 1987. "Why Have Minority Groups in North America Been Disadvantaged by Their Schools?" In *Education and*

Cultural Process: Anthropological Approaches, 2nd ed., ed. G. Spindler. New York: Holt, Rinehart and Winston.

————, eds. 1987. *The Interpretive Ethnography of Education: At Home and Abroad*. Hillsdale, NJ: Lawrence Erlbaum Associates.

Squire, J. R., and R. K. Applebee. 1968. *High School English Instruction Today*. New York: Appleton-Century-Crofts.

Stahl, S. A. 1985. "To Teach a Word Well: A Framework for Vocabulary Instruction." *Reading World* 24 (3): 16–27.

————. 1986. "Three Principles of Effective Vocabulary Instruction." *Journal of Reading* 29 (2): 662–68.

Stires, S., ed. 1991. *With Promise: Redefining Reading and Writing Needs for Special Students*. Portsmouth, NH: Heinemann.

Stonequist, E. 1937. *The Marginal Man: A Study in Personality and Cultural Conflict*. New York: Charles Scribner's Sons.

Taylor, D., and C. Dorsey-Gaines. 1988. *Growing Up Literate: Learning from Inner-City Families*. Portsmouth, NH: Heinemann.

Tharp, R., and R. Gallimore. 1989. *Rousing Minds to Life: Teaching, Learning, and Schooling in Social Context*. Cambridge, England: Cambridge University Press.

Trudgill, P. 1974. *Sociolinguistics*. New York: Penguin Books.

Trueba, H. 1987. "Organizing Classroom Instruction in Specific Sociocultural Context: Teaching Mexican Youth to Write in English." In *Becoming Literate in English as a Second Language: Advances in Research and Theory*, ed. S. Goldman and H. Trueba. Norwood, NJ: Ablex.

————. 1988a. "Culturally Based Explanations of Minority Students' Academic Achievement." *Anthropology and Education Quarterly* 19 (3): 270–87.

————. 1988b. "Peer Socialization among Minority Students, a High School Dropout Prevention Program." In *School and Society: Learning Content Through Culture*, ed. H. Trueba and C. Delgado-Gaitan. New York: Praeger.

————. 1989. *Raising Silent Voice: Educating the Linguistic Minorities for the Twenty-first Century*. New York: Harper and Row.

―――. 1990a. "Rethinking Dropouts: Culture and Literacy for Minority Student Empowerment." In *What Do Anthropologists Have to Say about Dropouts? The First Centennial Conference on Children at Risk*, ed. H. Trueba, G. Spindler, and L. Spindler. Basingstoke, New York: Falmer Press.

―――. 1990b. "The Role of Culture in Literacy Acquisition: An Interdisciplinary Approach to Qualitative Research." *Qualitative Studies in Education* 3 (1): 27–42.

Trueba, H., J. Lila, and E. Kirton. 1990. *Cultural Conflict and Adaptation: The Case of Hmong Children in American Society*. New York: Falmer Press.

Vygotsky, L. S. 1978. *Mind in Society*, ed. M. Cole et al. Cambridge, MA: Harvard University Press.

―――. 1986. *Thought and Language*, rev. and ed. Alex Kozulin. Cambridge, MA: The MIT Press.

Wattenmaker, B., and W. Virginia. 1980. *A Guidebook for Teaching English as a Second Language*. Boston: Allyn and Bacon.

Wong, F. L. 1982. "Instructional Language as Linguistic Input: Second Language Learning in Classrooms." In *Communication in the Classroom*, ed. L. Wilkinson. New York: Academic Press.

Zaharlick, A., and J. Green. 1991. "Ethnographic Research." In *Handbook of Research on Teaching the English Language Arts*, ed. J. Flood et al. New York: Macmillan.